Peter Ro

Poetry and Song in the works of J.R.R. Tolkien

Proceedings of The Tolkien Society
Seminar 2017

Edited by Anna Milon

First published 2018 by Luna Press Publishing, Edinburgh
www.lunapresspublishing.com

ISBN-13: 978-1-911143-49-9

Published under the auspices of the Peter Roe Memorial Fund, eighteenth in the series.

Contents

About the Peter Roe Memorial Fund

The Tolkien Society's seminar proceedings and other booklets are typically published under the auspices of the Peter Roe Memorial Fund, a fund in the Society's accounts that commemorates a young member who died in a traffic accident. Peter Roe, a young and very talented person joined the Society in 1979, shortly after his sixteenth birthday. He had discovered Middle-earth some time earlier, and was so inspired by it that he even developed his own system of runes, similar to the Dwarvish Angerthas, but which utilised logical sound values, matching the logical shapes of the runes. Peter was also an accomplished cartographer, and his bedroom was covered with multi-coloured maps of the journeys of the fellowship, plans of Middle-earth, and other drawings.

Peter was also a creative writer in both poetry and prose—the subject being incorporated into his own *Dwarvish Chronicles*. He was so enthusiastic about having joined the Society that he had written a letter ordering all the available back issues, and was on his way to buy envelopes when he was hit by a speeding lorry outside his home.

Sometime later, Jonathan and Lester Simons (at that time Chairman and Membership Secretary respectively) visited Peter's parents to see his room and to look at the work on which he had spent so much care and attention in such a tragically short life. It was obvious that Peter had produced, and would have continued to produce, material of such a high standard as to make a complete booklet, with poetry, calligraphy, stories and cartography. The then committee set up a special account in honour of Peter, with the consent of his parents, which would be the source of finance for the Society's special publications. Over the years a number of members have made generous donations to the fund.

The first publication to be financed by the Peter Roe Memorial Fund was *Some Light on Middle-earth* by Edward Crawford, published in 1985. Subsequent publications have been composed from papers delivered at Tolkien Society workshops and seminars, talks from guest speakers at the Annual Dinner, and collections of the best articles from past issues of *Amon Hen*, the Society's bulletin.

Dwarvish Fragments, an unfinished tale by Peter, was printed in *Mallorn* 15 (September 1980). A standalone collection of Peter's creative endeavours is currently being prepared for publication.

The Peter Roe Series

I	Edward Crawford, *Some Light on Middle-earth*, Peter Roe Series, I (Pinner: The Tolkien Society, 1985)
II	*Leaves from the Tree: Tolkien's Short Fiction*, ed. by Trevor Reynolds, Peter Roe Series, II (London: The Tolkien Society, 1991)
III	*The First and Second Ages*, ed. by Trevor Reynolds, Peter Roe Series, III (London: The Tolkien Society, 1992)
IV	*Travel and Communication in Tolkien's Worlds*, ed. by Richard Crawshaw, Peter Roe Series, IV (Swindon: The Tolkien Society, 1996)
V	*Digging Potatoes, Growing Trees: Volume One*, ed. by Helen Armstrong, Peter Roe Series, V (Swindon: The Tolkien Society, 1997)
VI	*Digging Potatoes, Growing Trees: Volume Two*, ed. by Helen Armstrong, Peter Roe Series, VI (Telford: The Tolkien Society, 1998)
VII	*Tolkien, the Sea and Scandinavia*, ed. by Richard Crawshaw, Peter Roe Series, VII (Telford: The Tolkien Society, 1999)
VIII	*The Ways of Creative Mythologies*, ed. by Maria Kuteeva, 2 vols, Peter Roe Series, VIII (Telford:

The Tolkien Society, 2000)

IX *Tolkien: A Mythology for England?*, ed. by Richard Crawshaw, Peter Roe Series, IX (Telford: The Tolkien Society, 2000)

X *The Best of Amon Hen: Part One*, ed. by Andrew Wells, Peter Roe Series, X (Telford: The Tolkien Society, 2000)

XI *Digging Potatoes, Growing Trees: Volume Three*, ed. by Helen Armstrong, Peter Roe Series, XI (Telford: The Tolkien Society, 2001)

XII Kenneth Chaij, *Sindarin Lexicon*, Peter Roe Series, XII (Telford: The Tolkien Society, 2001)

XIII *The Best of Amon Hen: Part Two*, ed. by Andrew Wells, Peter Roe Series, XIII (Telford: The Tolkien Society, 2002)

XIV *Tolkien: Influenced and Influencing*, ed. by Matthew Vernon, Peter Roe Series, XIV (Telford: The Tolkien Society, 2005)

XV *Freedom, Fate and Choice in Middle-earth*, ed. by Christopher Kreuzer, Peter Roe Series, XV (London: The Tolkien Society, 2012)

XVI *Journeys & Destinations*, ed. by Ian Collier, Peter Roe Series, XVI (Wolverhampton: The Tolkien Society, 2015)

XVII *Death and Immortality in Middle-earth*, ed. by Daniel Helen, Peter Roe Series, XVII (Edinburgh: Luna Press Publishing, 2017)

Conventions and Abbreviations

Citations to Tolkien's works are provided inline and use the following abbreviations. Because there are so many editions of *The Hobbit* and *The Lord of the Rings*, citations are by volume, book, and chapter only. Similarly, references to the appendices of *The Lord of the Rings* are by appendix, section, and subsection only. All other references are provided in footnotes according to the *MHRA Style Guide*. Bibliographies of all works consulted (other than Tolkien's works listed below) are found at the end of most chapters.

A&I	*The Lay of Aotrou and Itroun*, ed. by Verlyn Flieger (London: HarperCollins, 2016)
Arthur	*The Fall of Arthur*, ed. by Christopher Tolkien (London: HarperCollins, 2013; Boston: Houghton Mifflin Harcourt, 2013)
AW	*Ancrene Wisse* (Oxford: Oxford University Press, 1962)
B&L	*Beren and Lúthien*, ed. by Christopher Tolkien (London: HarperCollins, 2017)
Beowulf	*Beowulf: A Translation and Commentary, together with Sellic Spell*, ed. by Christopher Tolkien (London: HarperCollins, 2014; Boston: Houghton Mifflin Harcourt, 2014)
Bombadil	*The Adventures of Tom Bombadil and other verses from the Red Book* (London: George Allen &

Unwin, 1962; Boston: Houghton Mifflin, 1962)

CoH — *The Children of Húrin*, ed. by Christopher Tolkien (London: HarperCollins, 2007; Boston: Houghton Mifflin Harcourt, 2007)

Exodus — *The Old English Exodus*, ed. by Joan Turville-Petre (Oxford: Oxford University Press, 1982)

Father Christmas — *Letters from Father Christmas*, ed. by Baillie Tolkien (London: George Allen & Unwin, 1976; Boston: Houghton Mifflin, 1976)

FR — *The Fellowship of the Ring*

Hobbit — *The Hobbit*

Jewels — *The War of the Jewels,* ed. by Christopher Tolkien (London: HarperCollins, 1994; Boston: Houghton Mifflin, 1994)

Kullervo — *The Story of Kullervo,* ed. by Verlyn Flieger (London: HarperCollins, 2015; Boston: Houghton Mifflin Harcourt, 2016)

Lays — *The Lays of Beleriand,* ed. by Christopher Tolkien (London: George Allen & Unwin, 1985; Boston: Houghton Mifflin, 1985)

Letters — *The Letters of J.R.R. Tolkien,* ed. by Humphrey Carpenter with the assistance of Christopher Tolkien (London: George Allen & Unwin, 1981; Boston: Houghton Mifflin, 1981)

Lost Road	*The Lost Road and Other Writings*, ed. by Christopher Tolkien (London: Unwin Hyman, 1987; Boston: Houghton Mifflin, 1987)
Lost Tales I	*The Book of Lost Tales, Part One,* ed. by Christopher Tolkien (London: George Allen & Unwin, 1983; Boston: Houghton Mifflin, 1984)
Lost Tales II	*The Book of Lost Tales, Part Two*, ed. by Christopher Tolkien (London: George Allen & Unwin, 1984; Boston: Houghton Mifflin, 1984)
Monsters	*The Monsters and the Critics and Other Essays* (London: George Allen & Unwin, 1983; Boston: Houghton Mifflin, 1984)
Morgoth	*Morgoth's Ring*, ed. by Christopher Tolkien (London: Geore, 1993; Boston: Houghton Mifflin, 1993)
OFS	*Tolkien On Fairy-stories*, ed. by Verlyn Flieger and Douglas A. Anderson (London: HarperCollins, 2008)
P&S	*Poems and Stories* (London: George Allen & Unwin, 1980; Boston: Houghton Mifflin, 1994)
Peoples	*The Peoples of Middle-earth*, ed. by Christopher Tolkien (London: HarperCollins, 1996; Boston: Houghton Mifflin, 1996)
Perilous Realm	*Tales from the Perilous Realm* (London: HarperCollins, 1997)

RK	*The Return of the King*
Silmarillion	*The Silmarillion*, ed. by Christopher Tolkien (London: George Allen & Unwin, 1977; Boston: Houghton Mifflin, 1977).
Sauron	*Sauron Defeated*, ed. by Christopher Tolkien (London: HarperCollins, 1992; Boston: Houghton Mifflin, 1992)
Secret Vice	*A Secret Vice: Tolkien on Invented Languages*, ed. by Dimitra Fimi and Andrew Higgins (London: HarperCollins, 2016)
Shadow	*The Return of the Shadow*, ed. by Christopher Tolkien (London: Unwin Hyman, 1988; Boston: Houghton Mifflin, 1988)
Shaping	*The Shaping of Middle-earth*, ed. by Christopher Tolkien (London: George Allen & Unwin, 1986; Boston: Houghton Mifflin, 1986)
S&G	*The Legend of Sigurd and Gudrún*, ed. by Christopher Tolkien (London: HarperCollins, 2009; Boston: Houghton Mifflin Harcourt, 2009)
TL	*Tree and Leaf*, 2nd edn (London: Unwin Hyman, 1988; Boston: Houghton Mifflin, 1989)
TT	*The Two Towers*
Treason	*The Treason of Isengard*, ed. by Christopher Tolkien (London: Unwin Hyman; Boston: Houghton Mifflin, 1989)

UT	*Unfinished Tales of Númenor and Middle-earth*, ed. by Christopher Tolkien (London: George Allen & Unwin, 1980; Boston: Houghton Mifflin, 1980)
War	*The War of the Ring*, ed. by Christopher Tolkien (London: Unwin Hyman, 1990; Boston: Houghton Mifflin, 1990)

Introduction

Anna Milon

> Backwards and forwards swayed their song.
> Reeling and foundering, as ever more strong
> The chanting swelled, Felagund fought
> And all the magic and might he brought
> Of Elvenesse into his words.
> (*The Silmarillion, Of Beren and Luthien*)

The song duel between Finrod Felagund and Sauron is not the most often invoked instance of singing in Tolkien's writing, not when there are Galadriel's *Namarie*, Sam's plea to Elbereth and the whole of Ainulindale to draw upon. But it is, perhaps, the most obvious demonstration of the universality of song's magic. In the episode, the Elven king Finrod contests with the fallen Maia Sauron by what appears to be singing physical phenomena into life. Despite having no world-altering power, like the Valar, Finrod non-the-less creates through song.

At points of highest intensity in his writing, Tolkien resorts to verse, as the most potent form of narration, in deference to the oral poetic tradition of the ancient Nameless North with he had been enamoured since childhood. In his own words, 'blessed are the legend-makers with their rhyme' (*TL, Mythopoeia,* p. 88). However, poetry is treacherous as much as it is potent. According to Humphrey Carpenter, 'Tolkien … delayed drawing up a finished version of *The Silmarillion* … because he wanted to recast the two principal stories into verse.

… he regarded himself chiefly as a poet.'[1] However, Tolkien's reputation is not that of a celebrated poet, and *The Silmarillion* as it exists today is arguably very different from its creator's vision.

One of aforementioned principal stories, *The Lay of Leithian*, has been released as a separate publication in the Spring of 2017. Alongside the publication of *The Lay of Atrou and Itroun*, it reopens a space for discussing the place of poetry in Tolkien's fictional universe.

The present volume constitutes the proceedings of the annual Tolkien Society Seminar for the year 2017, held in Leeds on the 2nd of July. On the day, 10 speakers presented papers on the topic of poetry and song in Tolkien's writing and a further three engaged in a panel discussion on the recently published *The Lay of Atrou and Itroun*. Four of the papers are presented here. The first, by Massimiliano Izzo, explores the lesser-known poem 'The Song of Aelfwine' and the image of the Wandering Fire, a mesmerising will-o'-the-wisp. Following it, Kristine Larsen's paper addresses fires of a different kind: the annual revolution of stars above the Elven city of Kortirion in 'Kortirion among the Trees'. She examines Tolkien's masterful depiction of natural cycles in the poem. Szymon Pyndur discusses the parallels between versified oath-making in Kalevala and in the Silmarillion, with the notable example of Feanor's Oath. Finally, Bertrand Bellet discusses the challenges and rewards of translating Tolkien's verse into French and ways of forging stronger links between *The Lai of Atrou and Itroun* and the Breton lais that inspired it.

On behalf of the Tolkien Society, I extend most heartfelt

[1] Humphrey Carpenter, The Inklings (London: HarperCollins, 2006), p. 29.

gratitude to all the speakers for their contribution. I would also like to thank Daniel Helen for recording the presentations, and the Society committee at large for their prolonged support for this event.

In search of the Wandering Fire: otherwordly imagery in 'The Song of Ælfwine'

Massimiliano Izzo

In May 1924, J.R.R. Tolkien composed a poem entitled 'The Nameless Land' while he was reading the 14th century Middle English poem *Pearl* for examination purposes (*Lost Road*, p. 98). In its composition, Tolkien adopted *Pearl*'s stanza pattern with an extensive use of rhyme, alliteration, and assonance, as he aimed at demonstrating that the complex metrical form of *Pearl* could be used with reasonable success in Modern English (*Letters*, p. 317). The similarities are by no means limited to the style, but they extend to the subject treated. Just as in *Pearl*, in 'The Nameless Land' an unnamed narrator describes, using a visionary language with extensive use of adjectives, an ageless land akin to an earthly paradise and unaffected by the passing of Time. 'The Nameless Land' was published in 1927 in the anthology *Realities: an Anthology of Verse* and, like many of the poems published during his early years, never saw a second print.

Even so, Tolkien kept revising and rewriting it in the following decades. There exist five subsequent versions, according to Christopher Tolkien, and they underline a gradual but profound evolution in the conception of the poem. It was first renamed 'Ælfwine's Song calling upon Eärendel', and subsequently 'The Song of Ælfwine (on seeing the uprising of Eärendel)'. The narrator is never named in the poem itself, but from the title it becomes clear that he is now identified with Ælfwine the Mariner, the template elf-friend of Tolkien's legendarium. Of all the written revisions, two were published posthumously by Christopher Tolkien in *The Lost Road and Other Writings*. The first was marked by his father as an 'intermediate version' (actually the third revision), while the second is the final version (or the sixth revision). Based on the hypotheses drawn by Christopher Tolkien in his commentary to the poems, the intermediate version (from now on named 'The Song of Ælfwine I', *Lost Road*, pp. 100–102) dates from the middle 1930s and it could reasonably be coeval with the composition of the unfinished novel *The Lost Road*. Ælfwine the Mariner makes an apparition in one of the fragments that were conceived to be incorporated in the novel, as one of the many iteration of elf-friends in the history of England (and Western Europe more generally). In this fragment, set in the hall of King Edward, son of Alfred the Great, Ælfwine recites a poem on King Sheave, the mythological ancestor of King Hrothgar of Heorot. This fragment was never incorporated in the main narration of *The Lost Road*, but it would have been reused almost ten years later, when Tolkien tried once more to write a time travel/'scientifiction' story in the form of *The Notion Club Papers*. And it is quite possible, according to Christopher, that the final version, titled 'The Song of Ælfwine on seeing the uprising of Eärendil' (from now on called 'The Song of Ælfwine F', *Lost Road*, pp. 102–104), was written at the same time, though it could also belong to the period after the writing of *The Lord of the Rings*. In 'The Song of Ælfwine F' Eärendel has become Eärendil. The change of the name is first recorded in the first version of The Drowning of Anadûnê, whose evolution proceeded alongside *The Notion Club Papers*

(*Sauron*, p. 333). Therefore, this sets firmly the earliest possible date for the composition of 'The Song of Ælfwine F' as the same date of the composition of the *Notion Club Papers* in the middle 1940s. Regardless of the exact dates, it appears evident that there is a strong thematically connections between these works, as they both relate of possible voyages to or vision of the Otherworld by humans that acquire the status of elf-friend (at times, explicitly in their own name).

Poem structure and metre

Both 'The Nameless Land' and 'The Song of Ælfwine I' consist of 5 stanzas, each stanza being 12 lines long, for a total of 60 lines. The first two stanzas provide a description that highlights the enchanted and timeless quality of the Otherworld, mainly through the use of visual and auditory cues. There is a repeated contraposition between the world of mortal men ('here') and the ageless land ('there'). Nature there has a superlative quality, being 'more' than is here: grass is greener, trees are taller. The year is 'timeless', the morn 'unmeasured', and the evening is 'endless' and undimmed. For Tolkien, one of the most powerful qualities of fairy tales is their faculty to open a door to the Other Time, so that for a moment the reader lies outside of Time altogether (*OFS*, p. 48). This image is conveyed here, a vision of Faërie as a place free from the bonds of Time. This is the essence of its magic, or rather 'enchantment', to use Tolkien's preferred term from its inception in *On Fairy-stories*. This imagery is carried through in the first half of the second stanza with the references to 'glades for ever green' and 'immortal dew(s)'. The description acquires dynamism as the reader follows the musical plashing of fountain water flowing towards the 'Sea that no sail knows'. The first two stanzas end with a reference to the enigmatic 'wandering fire', which is named again in the first half-line of the following stanza (i.e. the second and the third). First the wandering fire is awakened, then it is blown to living flames, bringing light to the Land. The third stanza again puts the stress on the contraposition between 'here' and 'there', now focusing on the immeasurable distance and the impassable obstacles that will keep any mortal away: the lack of a steering star, the protection of the deep Night[1], untameable waters, and sheer shores. If the encircling obstacles are described as dark and drear, the Land itself is in contrast luminous thanks to cliffs of crystal and shining beaches. The fourth stanza offers the reader fleeting glimpses of the Land's inhabitants: unbraided hair, bare feet and lissom limbs, caught in some fleeting dance. No description can be provided in detail, because the loveliness of the Land's dwellers has never been contemplated by mortal man, even if one dared to sail 'the furthest Sea' or sought the 'unearthly winds behind the Sun'. In the final stanza, the poet offers two invocations, both filled with longing. The first is directed to the Land itself, referred variously through the use of metonymy as Shore and Haven[2]. Then the focus shifts from the Land to a star, seen by the poet rising in the west (more precisely, 'west of West'). The Star mirrors the Land in many aspects (the superlative brightness of its light, and its timelessness), and it is the object of the second

---

[1] The term 'Nether Night' is most likely a borrowing from William Morris's translation of Virgil's Aeneid, VII. 312, 324 <http://morrisedition.lib.uiowa.edu/aeneidtext.html#book_vii> [accessed 27 November 2017].

[2] The latter is most likely a reference to Avallónë, city and seaport of the Elves in Tol Eressëa, with which the Land will be explicitly identified in 'The Song of Ælfwine F' (see next section).

invocation, with which the poem terminates on a declamatory note.

The metrical pattern of the poem has been discussed in detail by Bonnet.[3] The unit element of the poem is a line: one line usually corresponds to a proposition. All the lines in the three published versions of the poem contain four stresses. The great majority of the lines are iambic tetrameters, an alternation of an unstressed and a stressed syllable. An anapaest (a foot consisting of two unstressed syllables followed by a stressed one) appears in roughly 10% of the lines. This metrical structure is analogous with *Pearl* whose metre has been described by Borroff as a 'iambic tetrameter varied by the occasional anapaest'[4]. The rhyme pattern can be summarised as follows: in a stanza 'two rhyme words alternate until the final four lines, which often work as a quatrain, where one of the rhymes (the latter) continues, and a counterpoint is picked up'[5]. This follows the rhyme scheme *ababababbcbc*. The second half of the final line in the first and second stanza is repeated on the following stanza — the second and the third, respectively. In all the three versions of the poem the repeated words refer, with small variation, to the "wandering fire(s)", making it an image of pivotal importance within the composition. Alliteration is used extensively throughout the poem, even though its role is ornamental rather than structural, once again mirroring the

[3] Bonet, Alain, *An Introduction to J.R.R.Tolkien's alliterative poetry*, (Paris: Paris IV Master Theses, 1996), pp. 28–30; 34–35.

[4] Borroff, Marie, *Pearl: a New Verse Translation* (New York: W.W. Norton, 1977), p. 32.

[5] Stanbury, Sarah, 'Introduction', *Pearl* (Kalamazoo: Medieval Institute Publications, 2001) <http://d.lib.rochester.edu/teams/text/stanbury-pearl-introduction> [accessed 26 November 2017].

approach of the *Pearl*-poet, a major model of the XIV–XV century Middle English alliterative revival. The alliteration patterns have been studied extensively by Bonnet.[6] Alliteration can happen only on stressed syllables; in the three version of the poem sixteen different consonant alliterative patterns can be found, using the phonemes /b/, /br/, /d/, /f/, /g/, /h/, /k/, /l/, /m/, /r/, /s/, /sh/, /st/, /t/, /v/, /w/. Vocalic alliteration occurs as well. Only one line in 60 has no alliteration in 'The Nameless Land', while all lines alliterate in 'The Song of Ælfwine F'. Some lines contain a double alliteration, such as line 12 of 'The Nameless Land', that alliterates according to the phonemes /w/ and /f/: "And the woods are filled with wandering fire.".

Evolution of the poem

The Nameless Land' as published in 1927, contained explicit references to Paradise and to Celtic or, more specifically, Irish folklore (*Lost Road*, pp. 98–100). The poem cites Bran mac Febail and Saint Brendan, protagonists of *imrama* or sea voyages to the Otherworld, and Tir-nan-Og, the Land of Youth, the most renowned of the Irish Otherworlds and dwelling of the Tuatha Dé Danann. There is also a single reference to Tolkien's legendarium, as developed in 'The Book of the Lost Tales': the Gnomish word Gondobar, known to be one of the names of Gondolin (*Lost Tales II*, p. 158). In the rewritings that brought us from 'The Nameless Land' to 'The Song of Ælfwine I' all the explicit references to Irish Folklore and to the medieval conception of Paradise were removed from the poem. Conversely, Tolkien started to introduce more words in his

[6] Bonet, pp. 30–33.

invented Elvish languages. The Land, that now has become 'of long forgotten name' rather than altogether nameless, is told to be the 'Land where still the Edhil are.' As of the middle 1930s, Edhil is not recorded as a Noldorin term. It is however found in its descendant Sindarin as the plural form of the word Edhel, cognate of the Quenya Elda, 'Elf, one of the star-folk' (*Jewels*, pp. 364, 374). The dwellers so fleetingly described in the fourth stanza seem them to be members of the Eldar, the High Elves who still dwell in the Blessed Realm and the island of Tol Eressëa after the end of the First Age and the destruction of Beleriand.[7] Further changes occurred between the intermediate and the final version. The fourth line is dropped out altogether and so the reader is denied any glimpse, however fleeting, of the mysterious inhabitants of the land. There is, however, an increase of references to Tolkien's legendarium, and usage of Elvish terms. The first one appears at the very beginning of the poem, in the form of the exclamation 'Eressëa! Eressëa!' right before the line 'There elven-lights still golden lie…'. The Land, now 'unknown by mortal name', is explicitly identified with Tol Eressëa, and the lights shining there are attributed to the Elves. In the second stanza of 'The Song of Ælfwine F' a 'dreaming niphredhil' — the flower known to be found in Doriath as well as on Cerin Amroth — grows as 'a star awakened'. In the final (now the fourth) stanza there is also a reference to 'the Tree', which most likely refers to Celeborn, the White Tree of Tol Eressëa, and the ancestor of the White Trees of Númenor and Gondor. The poem has thus been explicitly incorporated back in Tolkien's legendarium, even if it most likely belonged there

[7] Shippey, Tom, *The Road to Middle-earth*, 2nd edn (London: HarperCollins, 2012), p. 289.

since the beginning. For further discussion see Ekman.[8]

A short prose text and a 5-line alliterative poem — this one written in the Old English language and according to the Old English metre — act as a coda to 'The Song of Ælfwine F'. The prose piece contains a short account on Ælfwine and his sea travels. According to this text either he found the 'Straight Road' of the Elves to Eressëa, or, after long travels in the seas west of Ireland, he fell into a trance and was granted a vision of Eressëa before it was removed from the world. Afterwards, he was no longer able to rest in mortal lands, but had to sail again the western seas, aiming for the Undying Lands. The 5-line poem was allegedly pronounced by him before his final trip, from which he never came back. The same poem is present in *The Lost Road* (*Lost Road*, p. 44), and again attributed to Ælfwine Widlast ('the far-travelled'). It will reemerge once more in *The Notion Club Papers*, where Alwin Lowdham claims to 'have picked up echoes of some [...] lines' (*Sauron*, p. 244) and then proceeds reciting exactly the same poem as found in *The Lost Road* with the addition that Ælfwine Widlast is also called '*Eadwines sonu*', 'the son of Eadwine'.

Ælfwine in the context of the legendarium

Even though no traces of him survive in *The Silmarillion* as published, Ælfwine was for decades a central figure in the development of Tolkien's legendarium. He first appeared in the early 1920s in the tale 'Ælfwine of England' where he replaced Eriol the Mariner as the recipient of the stories of the Elves

[8] Ekman, Stephan, 'Echoes of Pearl in Arda's landscape', *Tolkien Studies 6* (Morgantown: West Virginia University Press, 2009), pp. 59–70.

recounted in 'The Book of the Lost Tales'. The original Anglo-Saxon name for Eriol was Ottor, but he also called himself *Wæfre*, 'restless, wandering' (*Lost Tales II*, p. 290). He was called a son of Eärendel, a he was "born under his beam" (i.e. the star's beam) (*Lost Tales II*, p. 290). The wandering characteristics of Eriol/Ottor are preserved in Ælfwine, who is called Luthien, 'wanderer', by the Fairies (*Lost Tales II*, p. 302). Ælfwine, as Eriol before him, represents the link between the Primary World — our Earth, and in particular North-western Europe in the X Century — and the Secondary World of Elvenhome and the Blessed Lands. He, an English man, was the receiver of the true tradition of the Fairies (Elves), about whom Irish and Welsh folks only tell garbled tales (*Lost Tales II*, p. 290). His role echoes that of many other characters that, throughout Tolkien's writings, act as a bridge between the mortal world of Men, and the Land of the immortal Elves. Elf-friends are such as Beren, Húrin Thalion, Bilbo, Frodo, Aragorn and Smith of Wootton Major. Within Tolkien's time-travel stories, the elf-friend's identity recurs throughout the ages in figures such as Elendil, Ælfwine the Mariner, Alboin Errol (in *The Lost Road*) and Alwin Arundel Lowdham (in *The Notion Club Papers*).

Just as 'The Song of Ælfwine' bears a strong Celtic flavour in its conception of the Otherworld that is kept even after the removal of explicit references, so does the figure of Ælfwine. He is said to be 'of England', but in the various accounts of his origin it is often stated that he has Celtic blood in his veins. In the original story 'Ælfwine of England' he is a son of a woman from Lionesse, Éadgifu (*Lost Tales II*, p. 313). Lionesse, called Evadrien ('the Coast of Iron') in Early Quenya (*Lost Tales II*, p. 313), was a legendary land located west of Cornwall that sunk into the sea after a cataclysm. Conversely, in *The Lost*

Road it is said that Ælfwine's wife 'was from Cornwall' (*Lost Road*, p. 84). In *The Notion Club Papers*, 'his mother has kin in the West Welsh' (*Sauron*, p. 270), that Christopher Tolkien identifies with the Cornish people again. It is moreover stated there that 'the lands of Welsh and Irish people are not stranger to him' (*Sauron*, p. 273).

The Wandering Fire

As seen in the previous sections, the pivotal image described in the poem is the one of wandering fire, acting as a link between subsequent stanzas. The sequence of the described events is the same in all the versions: as the evening approaches, over the music of the harp and the sound of a choir an unidentified voice awakens the fire in the woods. I reproduce here the last 4 lines of the fist stanza and the first 4 of the second from "The Song of Ælfwine I":

> When endless eve undimmed is near,
> o'er harp and chant in hidden choir
> A sudden voice upsoaring sheer
> in the wood awakes the Wandering Fire.
>
> The Wandering Fire the woodland fills:
> in glades for ever green it glows,
> In dells where immortal dew distils
> the Flower that in secret fragrance grows.
> (*Lost Road*, p. 101)

In the next link, between the second and the third stanza, a wind — said to be coming from beyond the world — blows on grass and bushes, bringing to living flame the fire previously awakened. Once again, from the intermediate version of the poem:

> Through gleaming vales it singing goes,
> where breathing keen on bent and briar
> The wind beyond the world's end blows
> to living flame the Wandering Fire.
>
> The Wandering Fire with tongues of flame
> with light there kindles quick and clear
> The land of long-forgotten name:
> no man may ever anchor near;
> (*Lost Road*, p. 101)

Now that the fire has been brought to full life, it illumines or kindles the land of the vision, so that it can be contemplated by the poet and he is able to describe its otherworldly beauty as best as he can. Tolkien does not explain what the wandering fire is, leaving the reader free to speculate on its meaning and its significance in the larger context of the legendarium. S. Ekman is the only author that, to the best of my knowledge, has proposed a solution: 'The "wandering fire" that ties together stanzas 1, 2, and 3 in the poem (lines 12–13 and 24–23 in all the three versions) is the mariner Eärendel who sails across the sky with a silmaril on his brow and his ship filled with divine flame (*Lost Road* 327; S250).'[9] I find this identification problematic in the light of the lines from the poem that I quoted above, and I do not think that the wandering fire is a direct reference to Eärendel in any of the published versions of the poem. There are at least two reasons for this. From the descriptions, the

[9] Ekman, pp. 62–63.

wandering fire 'fills the woodlands' and glows in glades and dells. This does not fit at all with a celestial body, though one could still surmise that the fire is the light of Eärendel, rather than the star itself. However, it seems safe to identify Eärendel with the 'wayward Star' referred by the narrator at the end of the poem. There is no ambiguity in this description as the Star is described as 'rising west of West' and as being located 'beyond the world'. It seems plausible that the Star is actually seen by Ælfwine not during his visit — or his vision — of Elvenhome and Eressëa, but rather once he has come back to the mortal lands. If this is the case — the poem is quite ambiguous in the temporal sequence of events, but the title actually points to this interpretation — then the longing and the memory of the timeless Land is brought back to Ælfwine, while he sees the star Eärendel rising in the west of 'Middle-earth' (possibly over the western ocean). This identification would seem in accord with the account given in the 'Quenta Silmarillion' as written in 1937, where Eärendel's ship Vingelot is sent by the Valar to soar the sky, as a beacon and a message of hope for the people of Beleriand and Middle-earth:

> Now when first Vingelot was set to sail on the seas of heaven, it rose unlooked-for, glittering and bright; and the folk of earth beheld it from afar and wondered, and they took it for a sign of hope. And when this new star arose in the West, Maidros said unto Maglor: 'Surely that is a Silmaril that shineth in the sky?' And Maglor said: 'If it be verily that Silmaril that we saw cast into the sea that riseth again by the power of the Gods, then let us be glad; for its glory is seen now by many, and is yet secure from all evil.' Then the elves looked up, and despaired no longer; but Morgoth was filled with doubt (*Lost Road*, pp. 327–28)

The idea, stated by Maglor, that the Silmaril carried by Eärendel is secure from all evil, is echoed in the final lines of the poem 'O! Star that shadow may not mar, nor ever darkness doom to die!' Having securely identified the Eärendel/Eärendil of the title with the Star of the final stanza, we must now try to solve the riddle of the wandering fire. A look into Tolkien's work in the first edition of the Oxford English Dictionary (OED) together with a study of previous occurrences of the term in English poetry can provide us some useful hints. This analysis takes flight from the undertaken by Rebekah Long and can be found in her Doctoral Thesis.[10] Tolkien contributed to many entries under the letter 'w', during his work for the OED in 1919 and 1920. According to Peter Giller, Tolkien personally wrote the entire cluster of words related to the verb *wander*, and his final versions were printed with little alterations, if any.[11] A section devoted to the expression 'wandering fire' is found at the entry for 'wandering', and this reads: 'Will-o'-the-wisp. (Now often fig. after Tennyson's use.)'. Three examples are shown, even though only two contain the term 'wandering fire', while a third one, a quotation from William Blake's *Songs of Innocence and Experience*, actually contains the synonym 'wand'ring light.'. The first and earliest quote is taken from Milton's *Paradise Lost*. There, the Serpent leading Eve towards the forbidden tree is compared to "a wandering fire, | compact of unctuous vapour, which the night | condenses, and

[10] Long, Rebekah, *Apocalypse and memory in Pearl* (Durham: Duke University Dissertations, 2005), pp. 262–67.

[11] Gilliver, Peter, 'At the wordface: J.R.R. Tolkien's Work on the Oxford English Dictionary', *Proceedings of the Tolkien Centenary Conference 1992* (Altadena, CA: Mythopoeic Press, 1995), p. 181.

the cold environs round, kindled through agitation to a flame"[12] that "hovering and blazing with delusive light, | misleads the amazed night-wanderer from his way | to bogs and mires, and of through pond or pool; | there swallow'd up and lost from succour far.".[13] Milton's description mirrors precisely the European folklore tradition of the *ignis fatuus* or will-o'-the-wisp:

> A meteoric light that sometimes appears in summer and autumn nights, and flies in the air a little above the surface of the earth, chiefly in marshy places near stagnant waters, and in churchyards. It is generally supposed to be produced by the spontaneous combustion of small jets of gas (carburetted or phosphuretted hydrogen) generated by the decomposition of vegetable or animal matter... Before the introduction of the general drainage of swamp-lands, the ignis fatuus was an ordinary phenomenon in the marshy districts of England.[14]

The *ignis fatuus* usually proceeds hovering or flying just above ground level. This behaviour agrees with the wandering fire as described by Tolkien in 'The Song of Ælfwine', which is dancing in the woodlands, glades, and dells rather than in marshlands. Both in folkloric tradition and in Milton's passage, the fire possesses a somewhat malevolent inclination, and leads wanderers astray from the safe way, and possibly to death in the bogs or mires. This deceitful behaviour is completely absent in Tolkien's poem. The evil and tricksy aspect of the

[12] Milton, John, *Paradise Lost*, IX. 634–36.

[13] Milton, IX. 639–43.

[14] Newell, William W., 'The ignis fatuus, its character and legendary origin'. *The Journal of American Folklore*, 17(64) (Champaign: University of Illinois Press, 1904), p. 42.

will-o'-the-wisp will appear yeas later in *The Lord of the Rings* as the candle-lights of the Dead Marshes (*TT*, IV, ii). The second quotation in the OED belong to Alfred Tennyson, who is also named in the entry itself. He used the term — always in plural form — in multiple occasions in *Idylls of the King*, as it has been reported by Long.[15] Here the depiction is even more figurative, and 'wandering fires' represent all the possible temptation that might lead astray the Knights bound to the Quest for the Holy Grail.

Tolkien removed the negative connotations when he wrote 'The Nameless Land', but he still retained the concept of the wandering lights. This closely mirrors a passage in the story of 'Ælfwine of England'. There, at the end of long journeys on the western Seas seeking in vain for the Blessed Land, Ælfwine and his seven fellow mariners travelling with him are surprised by a gentle breeze from the west and the sound of choirs and music like of harps, violins, and horns. They see a blue shadow afar, and they realise that they are in sight of the 'Haven of Many Hues':

> 'The night-flowers are opening in Faëry,' said Ælfwine; 'and behold,' said Bior, 'the Elves are kindling candles in their silver dusk,' and all looked whither his long hand pointed over their dark stern. Then none spoke for wonder and amaze, seeing deep in the gloaming of the West a blue shadow, and in the blue shadow many glittering lights, and ever more and more of them came twinkling out, until ten thousand points of flickering radiance were splintered far away as if a dust of the jewels self-luminous that Fëanor made were scattered on the lap of the Ocean.

[15] Long, pp. 263–67.

'Then is that the Harbour of the Lights of Many Hues,' said Ælfheah, 'that many a little-heeded tale has told of in our homes.' (*Lost Tales II*, p. 321)

'Ælfwine of England' was composed in 1920 or a few years later (*Lost Tales II*, p. 312). Together with the conception of Tol Eresseä in the same period, and the concomitant work of Tolkien on the OED, it could have provided a reasonable frame for the otherworldly descriptions of 'The Nameless Land' and the concept of the wandering fire(s). Notice how the expression 'the Elves are kindling candles' in the passage above will be echoed in a negative light by Gollum's sentence 'You should not look when the candles are lit.' (*TT*, IV, ii). In this sense, the Elvish lights, in contrast with the lights of the Dead Marshes, are not evil or tricksy *per se*, even though it would be perilous for mortals such Ælfwine to follow their guide and reach the shores of Faëry.

The discussion above clarifies at least the concept of the 'wandering fire(s)' in 'The Nameless Land'. However, in 'The Song of Ælfwine I' the wandering fire becomes capitalised as Wandering Fire and is always referred as a singular entity. Does this mark a change in its significance and importance? I would argue that it partly does and that the powerful life- and light-bringing quality of Tolkien's Fire in the poem bears little resemblance with the feeble and ephemeral will-o'-the wisp. To interpret this change better, it is helpful to examine one more poetic usage of the term, which was not recorded in the OED: the one authored by William Butler Yeats in the poem 'The Madness of King Goll.'[16] The lack of any reference to Yeats in

[16] Yeats, William Butler, *The collected poems of WB Yeats* (London: Random House, 1992), pp. 14–16.

Tolkien's writings, letters and notes is noteworthy, given the many interests that the two men shared: poetry, mythology and folk-lore, and the desire to relive or build a mythology for their respective nations. This silence is even more remarkable given that Yeats was held in high estimation by his fellow Inklings C.S. Lewis and Charles Williams. They both personally met the Irish poet in the 1920s-30s. Douglas A. Anderson, who studied the matter in the past, informed me that Yeats was also a major influence for the Tea Club, Barrovian Society (TCBS) member G.B. Smith, at least according to a review of *A Spring Harvest* by A.D. Burnett-Brown. 'If Yeats was a favourite of G.B. Smith before his death in December 1916, one might reasonably suspect that he communicated his enthusiasm to Tolkien.'[17] Unfortunately, the safest assumption remains that Tolkien was not acquainted with Yeats's work. Still, I consider useful to compare 'The Madness of King Goll' with 'The Song of Ælfwine', as they share many common elements: (1) a first-person narrator who is himself a poet, but is doomed to become a restless wanderer, (2) a Celtic, or rather Irish, background (more prominent in *King Goll*), and (3) the luring of an enchanted place or state of being whose best representation is given by the imagery of the 'wandering fire'. This term appears twice in Yeats's poem. First, when the madness is awakened in Goll during the frenzy of battle ('But slowly, as I shouting slew | And trampled in the bubbling mire, | In my most secret spirit grew | A whirling and a wandering fire'), and a second time when Goll manages to temporary quench is madness, after he finds a tympan, a stringed Irish musical instrument[18], which

[17] Douglas A. Anderson (personal communication).

[18] In the original version of the poem, Goll was to play a harp, rather than a tympan.

he plays to summon his muse Orchil.[19] Yeats had a personal preoccupation with madness, as he felt that it was transmitted generation through generation of his mother's family branch, the Pollexfens of Sligo.[20] He considered himself 'peculiar' and he felt that he had to keep this peculiarity under control through a strict discipline. Yeats's artistic output stems from a creative impulse that — he thought — if left unchecked, would have led him to insanity: 'I escaped from it as a writer through my sense of style. Is not one's art made out of the struggle in one's soul?'[21]. His identification with Goll, the narrator of the poem, was rather conscious: his father even used him as a model for a painting of the mad king.[22] In the light of this, the 'wandering fire' in 'The Madness of King Goll' can be seen as a figurative representation of creative impulse, that can lead to madness if not properly channeled through art (in the poem symbolised by the tympan and the muse Orchil). As a consequence of his madness, Goll becomes one with nature ('The grey wolf knows me; by one ear | I lead along the woodland deer; | The hares run by me growing bold.') and is cut off from the rest of humankind.[23] The ability to communicate with all the living creatures is one of the human desires ('ancient as the Fall') satisfied by the escapism of fairy-tales, according to Tolkien

---

19 Schuchard, Ronald, *The Last Minstrels: Yeats and the Revival of the Bardic Arts* (Oxford: Oxford University Press, 2008), p. 2.

20 Merrit, Henry. '"Under the moon": W.B. Yeats and the rhetoric of madness'. *Irish Studies Review* 4(16), (Abingdon-on-Thames: Routledge, 1996), p. 14–15.

21 Yeats, William Butler, *Memoirs*. Edited by Denis Donoghue (London: Macmilian, 1972), p. 157.

22 Similarly, Tolkien shows many points in common with his own narrator-poet cum wanderer, Ælfwine.

23 Merritt, p. 16.

(*OFS*, pp. 73 – 74). It can be seen an additional similarity with Tolkien's poems 'Looney' and its subsequent revision 'The Sea Bell', where the narrator, after a visit into Faerie, finds himself unable to communicate again with other people. Art, for King Goll, becomes the only restraint to madness, and it can only be achieved through the intercession of Orchil, that Yeats identifies as 'a Fomorian sorceress', and so a member of a supernatural race with connection to Faerie. The Fomorians were, according to Yeats, the progenitors of the leprechauns, one of the popular fairies of Ireland.[24]

Tolkien never appears concerned with madness in his writings, possibly also because he considered hallucinatory states incompatible with true fantasy (*OFS*. P. 60). However, the interpretation of the 'wandering fire' as a creative force can be applied with success to 'The Song of Ælfwine'. There are four relevant elements associated with the wandering fire scene in the poem: (1) the hidden choir, (2) the up-soaring voice, (3) the wind from beyond the world's end, and (4) the fire itself. Both wind and fire bear, in the Primary World as well as in Tolkien's secondary world, a figurative connection with the creative impulse, especially with the primitive creative impulse of the Creator, Eru Ilúvatar, as depicted in the early version of the *Ainulindalë* written in the early 1930s. The secret Fire, sent by Ilúvatar to burn at the heart of the World at the beginning of Time (*Lost Road*, p. 159) is the primitive representation of it in Tolkien's cosmology. The capitalisation of wandering fire in 'The Song of Ælfwine I' strengthen the idea of a connection between it and the Fire of Eru. To make a connection between

[24] Jeffares, A. Norman, *A Commentary on the Collected Poems of W.B. Yeats*. (Stanford, CA: 1968), p. 12.

the fire and the wind, it is necessary to consider the religious imagery that associates the Holy Spirit, the creative force of God in the Christian Bible, as both elements appears in the scripture of the Pentecost:

> And suddenly there came a sound from heaven as of a rushing mighty wind, and it filled all the house where they were sitting. And there appeared unto them cloven tongues like as of fire, and it sat upon each of them.[25]

In light of this passage, reading that 'the Wandering Fire hath tongues of flame' and that it was blown to living flame by a 'wind from beyond the world's end' acquires a stronger overtone. No explicit Christian message has to be assumed here to appreciate the description of the fire. Tolkien notoriously objected allegorical interpretations. However, it is worth to note that Ælfwine himself, an English man from the X century, was undoubtedly a Christian and familiar with the passage of the Pentecost. Tolkien wrote that Ælfwine was 'acquainted with Latin and, to some degree, with Irish'[26], which means that he most likely could read the Bible in the Latin vulgate. The reader can only speculate how allusive and intentional this description is, and whether it is necessary to add this external layer of interpretation. The capitalisation is removed again from the Wandering Fire in 'The Song of Ælfwine F', however it is consistently referred only in singular form. In this version, Tolkien altered the beginning of the third stanza to read: 'The

---

[25] Acts 2. 2–3, , King James Version.

[26] Tolkien, J.R.R., *Parma Eldalamberon no. 22: the Fëanorian Alphabet part I — Quenya Verb Structure*, ed. by Christopher Gilson and Arden R. Smith (Mountain View, CA: Parma Eldalamberon, 2015), p. 69.

wandering fire with quickening flame | Of living light illumines clear | That land unknown by mortal name' (*Lost Road*, pp. 102-3). The life-giving quality of the flame blown by the wind from beyond the world, echoes the quickening of a human soul from the breath of life[27], the creative Spirit of God: 'And so it written. The first man Adam was made a living soul. The last Adam a quickening spirit.'[28]

Some further considerations can be done concerning the voice and the hidden choirs, even though the connections are more tenuous. In any case, the word 'choir' is used rarely by Tolkien, but it appears consistently in reference to the Music of the Ainur, from the homonymous chapter in 'The Book of the lost Tales' to the various versions of the *Ainulindalë*. The voice, in its turn, brings to mind the act of Creation of the World by Eru, through the utterance of the word: 'Eä'. This event, appears only in the later versions of the *Ainulindalë*, from the second half of the 1940s. If all the four elements are considered together, the whole scene revolving around the wandering fire, appears evocative of an imagery reminiscent of the creative act in the *Ainulindalë*. It is the Fire, awakened by the voice — up-soaring over hidden choirs — and blown by the wind, that brings to life the Land — Elvenhome, Tol Eressëa — for the narrator (and the reader) to contemplate in its full splendour. In this light, the poem can be read as a visionary description of the (sub)creative act, and of the enchanted state experienced by the poet-narrator in accessing — through visit or vision — the ageless Land of the Edhil, 'sub-creators par excellence' (*Letters*, p. 146).

---

[27] Genesis 2. 7, King James Version.

[28] 1 Corinthians 15. 45, King James Version.

Works Consulted

Bonet, Alain, *An Introduction to J.R.R.Tolkien's alliterative poetry*, (Paris: Paris IV Master Theses, 2013).

Borroff, Marie, *Pearl: a New Verse Translation* (New York: W.W. Norton, 1977).

Ekman, Stephan, 'Echoes of Pearl in Arda's landscape', *Tolkien Studies* 6 (Morgantown: West Virginia University Press, 2009), pp. 59–70.

Fimi, Dimitra, 'Tolkien's 'Celtic' type of legends: merging traditions', *Tolkien Studies* 4 (Morgantown: West Virginia University Press, 2007), pp. 51–71.

Flieger, Verlyn, *Splintered Light. Logos and Language in Tolkien's Work*, 2nd edn. (Kent: The Kent State University Press, 2012).

Flieger, Verlyn, 'The footsteps of Ælfwine', *Green Suns and Fäerie*, (Kent: The Kent State University Press, 2012), pp. 74—88.

Gilliver, Peter, 'At the wordface: J.R.R. Tolkien's Work on the Oxford English Dictionary', *Proceedings of the Tolkien Centenary Conference 1992* (Altadena, CA: Mythopoeic Press, 1995), pp. 173–85.

Holdeman, David, *The Cambridge Introduction to WB Yeats* (Cambridge: Cambridge University Press, 2006).

Jeffares, A. Norman, *A Commentary on the Collected Poems of W.B. Yeats*. (Stanford, CA: 1968).

Long, Rebekah, *Apocalypse and memory in Pearl* (Durham: Duke University Dissertations, 2005).

Merrit, Henry. '"Under the moon": W.B. Yeats and the rhetoric of madness'. *Irish Studies Review* 4(16), (Abingdon-on-Thames: Routledge, 1996), pp. 14–17.

Milton, John. *Paradise Lost*, ed. by Philip Pullman (Oxford: Oxford University Press, 2005).

Newell, William W., 'The ignis fatuus, its character and legendary origin'. *The Journal of American Folklore*, 17(64), (Champaign: University of Illinois Press, 1904), pp. 39–60.

Schuchard, Ronald, *The Last Minstrels: Yeats and the Revival of the Bardic Arts* (Oxford: Oxford University Press, 2008).

Shippey, Tom, *The Road to Middle-earth*, 2nd edn (London: HarperCollins, 2012).

Stanbury, Sarah, 'Introduction', *Pearl* (Kalamazoo: Medieval Institute Publications, 2001) <http://d.lib.rochester.edu/teams/text/stanbury-pearl-introduction> [accessed 26 November 2017].

Tolkien, J.R.R., *Parma Eldalamberon no. 22: the Fëanorian Alphabet part I — Quenya Verb Structure*, ed. by Christopher Gilson and Arden R. Smith (Mountain View, CA: Parma

Eldalamberon, 2015).

Yeats, William Butler, *The collected poems of WB Yeats* (London: Random House, 1992).

——, *Memoirs*. Edited by Denis Donoghue, (London: Macmilian, 1972)

'Diadem the Fallen Day': Astronomical and Arboreal Motifs in the Poem 'Kortirion Among the Trees'

Kristine Larsen

As numerous authors have widely demonstrated, there are myriad astronomical allusions in the legendarium, from Tolkien's use of the phases of the moon to synchronize the chronology of *The Lord of the Rings* to Eärendil as the apparition of the planet Venus (the so-called Morning and Evening Star) in *The Silmarillion*. But Tolkien's astronomical references were not limited to his prose. Indeed, some of his most masterful and scientifically accurate borrowings appear in his poetry. While some of his poetic astronomical allusions are particularly obvious (such as the Man in the Moon poems and the hymn to Elbereth Gilthoniel), others are remarkable in their subtle scientific veracity. For example, as I have detailed elsewhere[1], in 'The Lay of Leithian' Tolkien's description of the Big Dipper (here called the 'Burning Briar') as behind Beren's back as he flees southward from Morgoth's allies is consistent with the real-world position of the asterism low in the North in the Autumn sky (*Lays*, pp. 167-68). Another excellent case in point is one of Tolkien's lesser known poems, 'Kortirion among the Trees' (also called 'The Trees of Kortirion'), written in 1915. It was revised in 1937 and again in the early 1960s

[1] Kristine Larsen, '"That sickle of the heavenly field": Celestial motifs in "The Lay of Leithian"', *Mallorn*, 54 (2013), 38-40.

(*Lost Tales I*, p. 32). The poem describes the seasonal changes seen in the city of Kortirion in Tol Eressëa in the earliest versions of the legendarium. The poem utilizes a number of accurate and clever references to astronomical and arboreal observations that reflect shifts in the natural world throughout the seasons, including the relative position of the Big Dipper, the Pleiades, and the full moon in the sky, as well as changes in the flowers and leaves of various tree species. This paper analyses a selection of these references.

While Tolkien's notes state that the poem was originally composed during 21-28 November 1915 in Warwick while on 'a week's leave from camp,' Christopher Tolkien cautions that letters sent to Edith at that time demonstrate that the poem was probably written in Rugeley Army Camp in Staffordshire (*Lost Tales I*, p. 32). The confusion possibly arose from the fact that Tolkien dedicated the poem to Warwick, where Edith Bratt resided (*Lost Tales I*, p. 25; *Letters*, p. 8). In one of the aforementioned letters, dated 26 November 1915, Tolkien explains to Edith that he wants to send a pencil copy to his close friends the T.C.B.S. [Tea Club and Barrovian Society] and later write out a 'careful ink copy' for her, but by the end of the letter he has changed his mind and sends the pencil copy to Edith and instead notes that he will 'keep the T.C.B.S. waiting till I can make another' (*Letters*, p. 8). The original poem is comprised of three main sections and a conclusion, although in the 1937 revision the conclusion is included within the third section. The length of the poem in its three versions is 140, 138, and 137 lines, respectively. Tolkien refers to the poem as 'so long' in the aforementioned letter to Edith, an ironic statement given the lengths of his later lays. The first section describes the now long-abandoned Elvish city in the Spring and early Summer, the second in the late Summer and early Autumn, and the third in late Autumn and Winter. These transitions are signalled to the reader by both the changes in the titular trees and the positioning of astronomical bodies in the sky. These literary clues are simultaneously both sophisticated and accessible to the reader, being naturally and seamlessly integrated into the poem, as well as drawing upon observations that the keen spectator and lover of nature (like Tolkien himself) would have certainly recognized. He also adds the occasional reference to the calendar month for those readers who spend less time observing the natural environment and would be less familiar with its seasonal shifts.

The title of the poem references trees in general, but within the body of the work several specific kinds of trees are described, including elms, maples, oaks, yews, and poplars. For this analysis, it is the elms that are of primary relevance, given that the Kortirion is located in 'the Land of Elms, Alalminórë in the Faery Realms' (*Lost Tales I,* p. 33, lines 21-22). When we first meet the trees of Kortirion, Tolkien in particular singles out the 'oaks, and maples with their tassels on', signifying the start of the poem as occurring in Spring (*Lost Tales I,* p. 33, lines 24). Both oaks and maples have impressive (and exceedingly messy for homeowners to clean up) yellow clumps of flowers that distribute their pollen. Videos posted on the website of the UK Woodland Trust document the annual changes in these trees, including their Spring 'tassels'.[2] The Spring setting is

[2] Woodland Trust, *Oak, English (Quercus robur)*, <https://www.woodlandtrust.org.uk/visiting-woods/trees-woods-and-wildlife/british-trees/native-trees/english-oak/> [accessed 4 October 2017]; Woodland Trust, *Maple, field (Acer campestre)*, <https://www.woodlandtrust.org.uk/visiting-woods/trees-woods-and-wildlife/british-trees/native-trees/field-maple/>

also signalled through the description of the Big Dipper in the night sky, seen through the evergreen branches of the yew trees. Tolkien notes that the 'seven lampads of the Silver Bear' (the seven bright stars of the Big Dipper) are seen to 'Swing slowly in their shrouded hair/And diadem the fallen day' (*Lost Tales I*, p. 33, lines 30-32). As a circumpolar constellation, Ursa Major (of which the Big Dipper is merely the brightest part) is always visible in the night sky from England, and is seen to slowly circle around Polaris, the North Star. In the Spring it is highest in the sky in the hours after sunset, and can be described, as Tolkien does, to crown or 'diadem the fallen day'. As Spring turns to Summer, or in Tolkien's words, 'bannered summer is unfurled,' it is the elms – 'Most full of music' – that take center stage, 'A gathered sound that overwhelms/ The voices of all other trees' (*Lost Tales I*, p. 33, lines 34-37). Elms are tall and majestic trees that have a full canopy of green leaves in the summer, what Tolkien terms 'their full sails' that are 'Like clothéd masts of verdurous ships' (*Lost Tales I*, p. 33, lines 39-40). Tolkien further describes the elms as ships sailing in a sea of grass, 'A fleet of galleons that proudly slips/ Across long sunlit seas' (*Lost Tales I*, p. 33, lines 41-42). This richly described summer tableau would certainly have been a familiar sight to Tolkien's intended readership.

The poem enters its second section, and with it the 'drowsy summer' (*Lost Tales I*, p. 34, line 55). Here the poet wistfully describes the passing of the too-brief English summer, and its 'rich-hued hours, th'enchanted nights' in which moths can be seen flying 'in the moveless air' (the stifling, breezeless Summer nights) as well as the 'radiant dawns,/ The fingered sunlight

---

[accessed 4 October 2017].

dripping on long lawns (*Lost Tales I*, p. 34, lines 67-71). On the Summer Solstice (or Midsummer's Eve) around June 21 of each year, the sun sets at about 9:30 PM and rises about 4:30 AM (8:30 PM and 3:30 AM without Daylight Saving Time) as seen from the middle of England, and the sky never gets completely dark (in the astronomical sense of the sun being at least 18 degrees below the horizon). These are 'th'enchanted nights' with 'rich-hued hours' of nearly perpetual twilight and the 'radiant dawns' that Tolkien speaks of. By meteorological summer (July), the length of the daylight hours is already decreasing, the nights are getting longer and darker, and the magic of these 'rich-hued hours' is rapidly disappearing. This is in keeping with the name of this second section in the 1960s revision of the work, Narquelion or 'Sun-fading', which Christopher Tolkien notes is the 'name of the tenth month in Quenya', i.e. our October (*Lost Tales I*, p. 41).

'Strange sad October' indeed quickly arrives, and as the year progresses toward All-Hallows Eve 'the wide-umbraged elm begins to fail;/ Her mourning multitudes of leaves go pale', a clear reference to the changing color of the elm's leaves from green to yellow (*Lost Tales I*, p. 34, lines 75-77). Tolkien attributes the mourning of the elms to their 'Seeing afar the icy shears/ of Winter' when the leaves will have been sheared from deciduous trees such as themselves (*Lost Tales I*, p. 34, line 79). Soon the elms realize that

> their hour is done,
> And wanly borne on wings of amber pale
> They beat the wide airs of the fading vale
> and fly like birds across the misty mere. (*Lost Tales I*, p. 34, lines 82-85)

As Mark Atherton assumes[3], the flight of the pale amber wings could refer to the falling of the leaves themselves, but it should be noted that the seeds of the tree, which are contained within a small winged fruit known as a samara, are also dispersed by the wind in Autumn.

The third section of the poem is termed Hrivion in the 1960s revision, the name derived from 'hrívë "winter"' (*Lost Tales I*, p. 42). It begins after All Hallows, in November, the time of the poem's composition, which the poet calls the 'season dearest to my heart,/Most fitting to the little faded town' (*Lost Tales I*, p. 35, lines 86-87). He notes that the 'late mornings are bejewelled with rime,' an apt description for cold frosty mornings in November when the sun rises several hours later than it had in June. But while the days are shorted and dreary, the nights are quite the opposite. Tolkien correctly calls the winter skies 'the season of the brilliant night,' (*Lost Tales I*, p. 35, line 97) as the winter skies feature more bright stars than other seasons (in the Northern Hemisphere).

Among the first of these to rise in the East are the Pleiades, the Seven Sisters, a star cluster in the constellation Taurus that is easily visible to the unaided eye. It is often confused with the Little Dipper, as its shape is reminiscent of that grouping. The Pleiades are referenced in the mythology and sacred texts of many Primary World cultures[4], including three citations in the Old Testament (Job 9:9 and 38:31, and Amos 5:8). The Pleiades are also widely mentioned in classic literature, from Manilius, Euripides, Hesiod and Homer through Milton and

---

[3] Mark Atherton, *There and Back Again: J.R.R Tolkien and the Origins of The Hobbit* (I.B. Tauris, 2014), pp. 102-103.

[4] Richard Hinckley Allen, *Star Names: Their Lore and Meaning* (New York: Dover, 1963), pp. 391-413.

Keats. Tolkien himself memorializes the rising of the Pleiades before Orion near midnight on a late September evening in *The Lord of the Rings* in the chapter 'Three's Company', writing 'Away high in the East swung Remmirath, the Netted Stars... and there leaned up, as he climbed over the rim of the world, the Swordsman of the Sky, Menelvagor with his shining belt' (*FR*, I, iii). The cluster is visible in the eastern sky in early evening in November, and in 'Kortirion among the Trees' it is said that the 'naked elms entwine in cloudy lace/ The Pleiades' (*Lost Tales I*, p. 35, lines 98-99). This image of the stars seen through the leafless trees as being encased in lace is reminiscent of Alfred Lord Tennyson's 'Locksley Hall', where the poet reminiscences that "Many a night I saw the Pleiads, rising thro' the mellow shade,/ Glitter like a swarm of fire-flies tangled in a silver braid'[5]. An older reference of the same type is found in the thirteenth century Persian poem 'Rose-Garden' by Sadi, where it is said that the 'necklaces of Pleiades seemed to hang upon the branches of the trees'[6]. In Finnish and Lithuanian folklore the Pleiades are seen as 'a Sieve with holes in it' while in French folklore it is likened to a mosquito net.[7] Seen in this context, Tolkien's later name for the cluster, Remmirath, the Netted Stars, is both consistent with Real World mythology and perhaps motivated by his depiction of it in 'Kortirion among the Trees'. But the reference to the Pleiades in this poem contains another seasonal astronomical allusion as well. The 1937 version of the verse reads in full

---

[5] Alfred Tennyson, *Poems, vol. II* (Boston: William D. Ticknor, 1842), p. 93.
[6] Robert Burnham, *Burnham's Celestial Handbook, vol. 3* (New York, Dover, 1978), p. 1864.
[7] Allen, p. 397.

> When naked elms entwine in branching lace
> The Seven Stars, and through the boughs the eye
> Stares golden-beaming in the round moon's face. (*Lost Tales I*, p. 38, lines 97-99)

The 'round moon' is the full moon, which passes through Taurus and appears near the Pleiades (the 'Seven Stars' or Seven Sisters) in the sky in late November or early December.

The next lines of the poem are particularly melancholy, urging the 'fading fairies and most lonely elves' to sing in their grief and 'Remember what is gone – /The magic sun that lit Kortirion!'(*Lost Tales I*, p. 35, lines 101-107). Both the sorrowful state of the fairies and the loss of the magic sun are further explained in a prose introduction that Tolkien appended to the poem, where it is said that

> on a time the great Faring Forth [to rescue the Elves that had been lost in the Great Lands East of the Great Sea] was made, and the fairies had rekindled once more the Magic Sun of Valinor but for the treason and faint hearts of Men. But so it is that the Magic Sun is dead and the Lonely Isle drawn back unto the confines of the Great Lands, and the fairies are scattered through all the wide unfriendly pathways of the world; and now Men dwell even on this faded isle, and care nought or know nought of its ancient days. (*Lost Tales I*, p. 25)

The Magic Sun is the golden tree Laurelin as the progenitor of the actual Sun, which in *The Book of Lost Tales* is the last flower of Laurelin as a lamp that is directed across the sky (similar to the Moon as the last flower of the silver tree Telperion, originally called Silpion). The sun later becomes the last fruit of Laurelin in the *Silmarillion* texts. This is one of the earliest references to the Two Trees of Valinor in the legendarium, but earlier still by several months are the poem 'The Shores of Faëry' (written in mid 1915) and the painting of the same name, which Wayne Hammond and Christina Scull report is dated May 10, 1915.[8]

A final arboreal/astronomical reference to the seasons in Kortirion is found near the end of the third section, in the dead of winter when 'Bare are thy trees become, Kortirion,/ And all their summer glory swiftly gone' (*Lost Tales I*, p. 35, lines 119-20). In contrast to the waning of the trees, Tolkien notes that

> The seven lampads of the Silver Bear
> Are waxen to a wondrous flare
> That flames above the fallen year. (*Lost Tales I*, p. 39, lines 121-23)

The 'seven lampads of the Silver Bear' are the seven bright stars of the Big Dipper, again the brightest stars of Ursa Major, the Great Bear. As previously described, the Big Dipper does not set as seen from England, and instead circles around the North Star over both the course of the night and the progress of the seasons. While it is low in the Northern sky in Autumn, by Winter it is beginning to rise, or wax, in the evening sky, and is seen standing upright on its handle to the East (right) of the North Star. In this position, with the bowl of the dipper seen poised on the top of the handle, it can be said to resemble a large candle flame 'waxen to a wondrous flare/ That flames above the fallen year'.

It is fitting that the poem ends in the dead of winter, when

---

[8] Wayne G. Hammond and Christina Scull, *J.R.R. Tolkien: Artist and Illustrator* (Boston: Houghton Mifflin, 2000), pp. 47; 66.

the year has faded, symbolizing the fading of the Elves in the 'Land of withered Elms' (*Lost Tales I*, p. 36, line 136). But there is another, Primary World sense, in which the poem is hauntingly prophetic. Due to Dutch elm disease, the beloved elms of England, like those of Kortirion, are dying. The fungal disease spread by bark beetles began to ravage the trees of England after World War I, and has continued to wreak havoc in waves of activity to the present day.[9] To Tolkien, who described himself as 'much in love with plants and above all trees' (*Letters*, p. 220), this would have seemed not only tragic, but a fitting symbol of Arda Marred – Morgoth's Ring, as it were – the fallen world in which we live. As Tolkien ends his introductory note to the poem, 'Think on Kortirion and be sad – yet is there not hope?' (*Lost Tales I*, p. 26). In terms of the trees of England, there is. For while an adult English elm tree falls victim to the disease, some of its roots survive, and spawn a new generation of trees.[10] Therefore, in the dead of winter, when we look upon the Big Dipper, standing as a flaming candle in the North, perhaps we should consider it to be, as Tolkien suggested, a beacon of hope, signifying that both the Magic Sun and the elms of England may, one day, be rekindled. Then, perhaps, we can at least imagine that the Elves will return to the forlorn byways of Kortirion among the Trees.

---

[9] Forestry Commission, *Dutch elm disease (Ophiostoma novo-ulmi)* (2017), <https://www.forestry.gov.uk/dutchelmdisease> [accessed 5 October 2017].
10. Forestry Commission, *Dutch elm disease (Ophiostoma novo-ulmi)*.

Works Consulted

Allen, Richard Hinckley, *Star Names: Their Lore and Meaning* (New York: Dover, 1963).

Atherton, Mark, *There and Back Again: J.R.R Tolkien and the Origins of The Hobbit* (London: I.B. Tauris, 2014).

Burnham, Robert, *Burnham's Celestial Handbook, vol. 3* (New York, Dover, 1978).

Forestry Commission, *Dutch elm disease (Ophiostoma novo-ulmi)* (2017), <https://www.forestry.gov.uk/dutchelmdisease> [accessed 5 October 2017].

Hammond, Wayne G. and Christina Scull, *J.R.R. Tolkien: Artist and Illustrator* (Boston: Houghton Mifflin, 2000).

Larsen, Kristine, '"That sickle of the heavenly field": celestial motifs in "The Lay of Leithian"', *Mallorn*, 54 (2013) 38-40.

Tennyson, Alfred, *Poems, vol. II* (Boston: William D. Ticknor, 1842).

Woodland Trust, *Maple, field (Acer campestre)*, <https://www.woodlandtrust.org.uk/visiting-woods/trees-woods-and-wildlife/british-trees/native-trees/field-maple/> [accessed 4 October 2017].

Woodland Trust, *Oak, English (Quercus robur)*, <https://www.woodlandtrust.org.uk/visiting-woods/trees-woods-and-

wildlife/british-trees/native-trees/english-oak/> [accessed 4 October 2017].

The Magical and Reality-Transforming Function of Tolkien's Song and Verse

Szymon Pyndur

I would like to begin with a quote from *The Lord of the Rings*: 'Even as they stepped on the threshold a single clear voice rose in song [...] [Frodo] stood still enchanted, while the sweet syllables of the elvish song fell like clear jewels of blended words and melody' (*FR*, II, I). This is when the hobbits are leaving the Hall of Fire in the house of Elrond and hear the hymn *A Elbereth Gilthoniel.*

A vital thing to stress here is the enchantment that the song causes and the way it influences Frodo. Its magical nature makes Frodo stop and listen as if he were bound and unable to move. The song is able to affect the reality in some way, and I daresay that the light of that quote shines through the whole body of Tolkien's work.

In Tolkien's stories, we can find a strong conviction that words have power. The language is a very powerful tool that has to be used with the utmost caution. That can come as no surprise, as Tolkien was a prominent philologist.

There are of course different ways of using language and different forms of it. But perhaps the most perfect and beautiful application of language is a poem. The ability to work the words into the strict rules of rhyme and rhythm is a truly marvellous thing. I think that we could all agree that a well written poem indicates a proficient language user. Words of such a masterpiece when blended with a beautiful and enchanting melody (as Tolkien writes in the aforementioned quote) combine together for a very powerful and influential blend. A blend so powerful that it can sometimes even affect physical reality. Its beauty enchants us and sometimes even manipulates. That would explain why many spells often come in a form of songs and incantations.

In Tolkien's legendarium, the power of a song to affect the physical reality has been very significant since the very beginning of things, as the whole world was created through singing. That reality-transforming nature of songs can be seen in numerous instances throughout the whole history of Middle-Earth. However, Tolkien's works, as ingenious as they are, are not the sole place where we can find such nature and employment of songs.

I am talking here about the *Kalevala* – Finnish mythological folk songs compilation by which Tolkien was greatly inspired, as we know from his venture into its world, namely *The Story of Kullervo* and its latter significance for the whole Middle-Earth legendarium and its development.

In the *Kalevala*, being entirely composed of songs, songs and language have a very important role ascribed to them. A song is associated with wisdom and knowledge and perceived as a powerful tool that can affect the reality. If one has knowledge about a certain thing he has power over it. In fact, the wisest and most powerful being in the *Kalevala*, its main hero – Väinämöinen, is a wizard and a chanter of songs. Using his songs, he can affect the reality in many ways.

Singing in the *Kalevala* has a powerful magical significance. Songs are often used as spells, charms and prayers. What is interesting is the fact that such a vital role of songs can hardly be found in other mythologies of northern Europe. That is why the *Kalevala* is very likely to have had a tremendous influence on Tolkien in that matter.

In both Tolkien's works and the *Kalevala* we can distinguish several forms of verse that has a magical power to it. These are respectively: an oath, a curse, a spell or prayer and finally the most exciting and original one – the song duel. In all of these, the power of song to affect reality works in slightly different ways. I am going to present examples of all these forms found in the *Kalevala* and Tolkien and briefly examine the stylistic and linguistic devices used in them.

The first form I would like to talk about is an oath. We can find a great example of that form in Tolkien's *Oath of Fëanor* which I quote here in full:

> Be he foe or friend, be he foul or clean,
> brood of Morgoth or bright Vala,
> Elda or Maia or Aftercomer,
> Man yet unborn upon Middle-earth,
> neither law, nor love, nor league of swords,
> dread nor danger, not Doom itself,
> shall defend him from Fëanor, and Fëanor's kin,
> whoso hideth or hoardeth, or in hand taketh,
> finding keepeth or afar casteth
> a Silmaril. This swear we all:
> death we will deal him ere Day's ending,
> woe unto world's end! Our word hear thou,
> Eru Allfather! To the everlasting
> Darkness doom us if our deed faileth.
> On the holy mountain hear in witness
> and our vow remember, Manwë and Varda!
> (*Morgoth*, p. 112)

This piece of verse has perhaps the greatest impact on the narrative of the *Silmarillion*. It has a tremendous power due to its careful construction and various elements that enhance its potency. The structure of this oath is very similar to those found in the *Kalevala*. In this particular case, the oath of Lemminkainen and Kyllikki, his future wife, a part of which I quote here. The oath is that Lemminkainen will not leave her and go to war and Kyllikki will not ever go to the village to dance with other girls.

> "Here I swear, by oaths eternal,
> Not again to join in battle,
> Whether love of gold may lure me,
> Or my wish is fixed on silver.
> But thyself on oath must pledge thee,
> Not to wander to the village,
> Whether for the love of dancing,
> Or to loiter in the pathways."
> Then they took the oaths between them,
> And with oaths eternal bound them,
> There in Jumala's high presence,
> In the sight of the Almighty,
> Ahti should not go to battle,
> Nor should Kylli seek the village.
> (*Kalevala, Runo XI*, lines: 301-314)

Looking briefly at the structure of them, in both cases there are some preemptive conditions, factors that may disrupt the oath's execution and on the other hand conditions that may lead to it. In the *Oath of Fëanor* the conditional part is very complex and extensive, it includes all of the first nine lines of the oath. We can find there both the disruptive and supportive factors.

In the *Kalevala*, the conditional part is shorter as it is only two lines, those are: 'Whether love of gold may lure me, Or my wish is fixed on silver'. In this case, these are only factors that can disrupt the oath's execution.

Then we have something that may be called an oath 'carrier' being an immediate lead-up to the main proposition of the oath and its very content intensifying the weight of what is to be said next. In the *Oath of Fëanor* it is the expression: 'This swear we all...' The presence of the adjective 'all' intensifies the expression and somehow underlines it. In the case of *Kalevala*, it is: "Here I swear, by oaths eternal..." where the oath is intensified and actually presented as such with the words 'by oaths eternal', with the adjective 'eternal' as an intensifier.

Couple of things worth noting here are the usual verbs used in that part, such as 'swear' or 'pledge' which can hardly be substituted by anything. Another point here is that this introductory part actually makes an oath. Without it, we could not call it so.

What comes next is the effective part of the oath which includes the oath's main propositional value and the effects that are going to have place when the oath's conditions occur. The expressions are usually very formal and 'pompous' in a sense. A lot of archaic language, exclamations and stylistic inversion is used. In the 'Oath of Fëanor' it is: 'death we will deal him ere Day's ending, woe unto world's end!' In the *Kalevala*, it is: 'Not again to join in battle', a little bit shorter, but still ceremonial, with the relocation of the adverb 'again'.

What follows next is usually an invocation to a higher power or a divinity, a plea for strength to make the oath's execution possible, and strengthen it. There are many apostrophes and flattering epithets in order to gain the divinity's favour. In the case of the 'Oath of Fëanor' it is Eru Allfather along with two of the Valar – angelic beings – Manwë and Varda. There is also a request for a divine punishment in case of failure as an additional preemptive measure. In the case of *Kalevala*, the divinity's presence is only mentioned after the oath and is not invoked directly, which makes the oath considerably weaker.

Now I would like to move to the next form, namely a curse. I will present here a versified curse uttered by the smith Asemo's wife in *The Story of Kullervo*, being a direct adaptation of the *Kullervo Cycle* from the original *Kalevala*. An interesting fact is that it only exists as a fully developed curse in Tolkien's adaptation, where the smith's wife, on the verge of death curses the main character Kullervo and says that his end shall be even more terrible than his hapless life up to that time:

Ill thy fortune dark thy faring
On the roadway of thy lifetime.
Thou has trod the ways of thralldom
And the trackless waste of exile
But thy end shall be more awful
And a tale to men forever
Of a fate of woe [and] horror
Worse than anguish in Amuntu.
Men shall hither come from Loke
In the mirklands far to northward
And shall hither come from Same
In the southways of the summer
And shall fare to us from Kēme
And from the Ocean bath to Westward
But shall shudder when they hear them
Thy fate and end of terror.
To woe thou who as [illegible] (*Kullervo*, pp. 31-32)

In the Kalevala it is not an outright curse, but rather a prayer to God (Ukko) to kill Kullervo with a dart from his crossbow. So it also bears traits of an ill wish. It goes as follows:

> Then said Ilmarinen's housewife,
> "Ukko, thou, of Gods the highest,
> Haste to bend thy mighty crossbow,
> Of thy bows the best select thou,
> Take thou then a bolt of copper,
> And adjust it to the crossbow,
> Shoot thou then a flaming arrow,
> Shoot thou forth the bolt of copper,
> Shoot it quickly through the arm-pits,
> Shoot it that it split the shoulders.
> Thus let Kalervo's son perish,
> Shoot thou dead this wicked creature,
> Shoot him with the steel-tipped arrow,
> Shoot him with thy bolt of copper."
> (*Kalevala, Runo XXXIII*, lines: 263-276)

The version from the *Kalevala* is a simple invocation to a divinity, an apostrophe with the aforementioned flattering and praising epithets. 'Ukko, thou, of Gods the highest, Haste to bend thy mighty crossbow...' So, the reality-transforming power of the verse itself relies here on the will and power of a divinity, and it accomplishes that through the usage of an apostrophe. This is the way the language works basically in every prayer.

In Tolkien's version of the curse, the element of an invocation to a higher power is not present at all. The words are spoken directly to the affected entity, that is, Kullervo, and the sole fact of uttering them is meant to have a reality-changing power. So, the power lies entirely in the words of the song. We have some comparisons of the fate of Kullervo to the most terrible horrors, such as anguish in Amuntu, which is an equivalent of hell. An interesting thing to notice is also the fact that the more elevated the language gets, the stronger the curse appears to be.

Now we will move on to another form, which is a spell or a prayer. I am saying 'or', because the fact whether it is one or another is determined by which entity is being addressed. If it is a divinity that is asked to do something for the implorer, then it is a prayer and if it is the being that the words are meant to directly affect, then it is a spell.

Examples here would be the prayers and charms for the protection of cattle sung by the smith's wife in Runo XXXII of the *Kalevala* and the Tolkienian counterpart of that fragment of verse found in *The Story of Kullervo*. Due to the length of both these texts I will not quote them here in full, citing only the parts relevant to my analysis.

In both of them we can find a prayer, as there are invocations to Ukko the god, and numerous spirits of the forest to ensure that they protect cattle during pasture. Tolkien does not copy the spirits of the forest, but invents some of his own. And later there is also an example of a spell in the form of a charm addressed to a bear, so that it does not do any harm to the cattle. Very frequent poetic devices are flattering expressions and epithets, obviously, apostrophes and the typical for *Kalevala* style extensive use of parallelism in the description. For example: 'In the fine days of the summer, In the good Creator's summer, In the days of Ilu's laughter.' (*Kullervo*, pp. 22-27). All these things can be found in the original song and in Tolkien's adaptation as well. The so called 'cattle song' from the *Kalevala* is very long and that perhaps gives some power to its words as well, as it is nearly five hundred lines long and it would be impossible to analyse it in detail here. But it is surely a tremendous piece of verse.

Having said all this, I would like to move to the perhaps most exciting form, namely the song duel which I would like to analyse here in greater detail than the other forms. A song duel is a situation in which two singers fight each other exclusively by singing. It is original for the *Kalevala* and it hardly ever features in other mythologies and literary works. Such a duel in the Kalevala is conducted between two great singers: Väinämöinen – the greatest magician and Joukahainen – a young and somewhat presumptous singer of songs (*Kalevala, Runo III*, lines: 1-580).

Tolkien, possibly influenced by the *Kalevala*, uses this motive in his *Lay of Leithian* where Sauron challenges Felagund to compete with him through song. In both cases the songs are very powerful and have a tremendous impact on the singers, affecting them even in physical terms. Let us now take a closer look at both duels and see the patterns that are employed in them.

I will start with the *Kalevala* and the duel between Väinämöinen and Joukahainen. The story of it is told in the Runo III of the *Kalevala*. I am going to summarize it now for the sake of brevity. It begins with the circumstances that lead to the duel. We have a description of Väinämöinen and his fame and mastery in singing songs. We encounter here the idea that songs are wisdom, which is very frequent in the *Kalevala*. We read that Väinämöinen: 'Sang the songs of by-gone ages, Hidden words of ancient wisdom' (*Kalevala, Runo III*, lines: 9-10). So his proficiency in singing indicates his great knowledge and experience.

Then follows a description of Joukahainen and his envy for Väinämöinen's wisdom. (ibid., lines: 31-40) We can see here a strong antithesis in the description of the two characters. Väinämöinen is described as 'old and steadfast' which is his permanent attribute in the whole *Kalevala*, as in the famous Finnish lines: 'Vaka Vanha Väinämöinen'. Whereas Joukahainen is described as 'youthful'. It is a trait of another *Kalevalian* conviction that old age implies wisdom. Going with that line of reasoning we can easily arrive at the idea that if songs are wisdom then old age must imply also proficiency in song. Which is quite reasonable to think, as in the Finnish folk tradition, songs were sung by the elders.

But going back to the narrative, we learn that Joukahainen goes searching for Väinämöinen to prove that he is a better minstrel than him and he bumps into him by chance, driving his sledge. When they learn their names, Joukahainen challenges Väinämöinen to a song duel. So Väinämöinen asks him what he knows (ibid., lines: 144-146). Thus we encounter again the *Kalevalian* 'song = wisdom' equation. Joukahainen starts to sing, but he sings about obvious and simple things, that do not seem to be particularly hard to know, like for example: 'In the roof we find a smoke-hole, And the fire is near the heartstone' (ibid., lines: 151-152). Väinämöinen listens to all that and constantly mocks him: 'Childish tales and women's wisdom, but for bearded men unsuited [...] tell me words of deepest wisdom' (ibid., lines: 184-188). Joukahainen tries to sing of more weighty things, but it is ineffective, so he starts to lie, ascribing to himself some of the primeval roles of creation, that he could not have had. As we know: A lie has no legs. In fact, the words of Joukahainen do not have any power and Väinämöinen knows that.

At that point Väinämöinen gets angry and starts singing himself. He sings of eternal, primeval things, of deepest wisdom. It immediately affects reality, as we read 'Lakes swelled up, and earth was shaken...' (ibid., lines: 296-300). Väinämöinen starts to change Joukahainen's possessions into pieces of surrounding nature, and then starts literally singing Joukahainen into a swamp, so powerful are his songs. The duel ends with Joukahainen on the verge of drowning, begging Väinämöinen to release him from his singing and promising him different things in exchange for his own sister to be his wife. And finally, Vainamoinen agrees (ibid., lines: 301-470). The whole duel is a theatre of antithesis, with *old* Väinämöinen singing of eternal and primeval things and *youthful* Joukahainen singing of ordinary, obvious and unimportant things which leads to the former's overwhelming victory.

Just such a duel is carried out by Tolkien in the duel between Sauron and Felagund, a version of which is included in the *Silmarillion*. In the duel we also encounter a lot of antithetical imagery. Felagund sings about 'freedom, trust, escape' whereas Sauron sings about 'treachery, piercing and betraying' (*Silmarillion*, p. 171). A thing of great importance is the context. It is the situation when Sauron wants to reveal the identity of Felagund, Beren and their companions, while they are trying to conceal it from him.

The accumulation of antithetical imagery in the songs increases tension tremendously. They collide with the power of enormous waves. In the next part Felagund sings about beautiful images: 'Softly in the gloom they heard the birds | Singing afar in Nargothrond | The sighing of the Sea beyond | Beyond the western world, on sand | On sand of pearls in Elvenland' (ibid.). Sauron sings about entirely different things:

‘Then the gloom gathered; darkness growing | In Valinor, the red blood flowing | Beside the Sea, where the Noldor slew | The Foamriders, and stealing drew Their white ships with their white sails | From lamplit havens. The wind wails, | The wolf howls. The ravens flee. | The ice mutters in the mouths of the Sea. | The captives sad in Angband mourn. Thunder rumbles, the fires burn’ (ibid.). The most important fact is that Sauron sings the truth about Felagunds kin, the dark truth about their evil deeds, such as the kinslaying in Alqualonde. That is the knowledge that Sauron employs in his fight against Felagund, and through this knowledge he manages to overcome him, as he hits him in his *Achilles’ heel*. Finally, we see accumulation of Sauron’s dark imagery: the wolves howling and so on and we feel that Felagund’s power dwindles. The effect is so strong that it has physical impact over Felagund as he falls to the ground and thus Sauron wins the duel (ibid.).

To sum up both duels, we can see how the game of oppositions works in both of them, this is the core feature of a song duel, two entirely different perspectives colliding. The victory in such a duel depends on who is in fact the greatest poet, and who is able to strengthen his imagery enough to prevail over the other.

Thus can be seen the different forms of verse through which the reality is changed and that have a magical function in the Kalevala, as well as Tolkien’s works. Also vital is the role of singers and chanters of songs in both those worlds and the numerous ways they affect the reality of the narratives. They participate, in some sense, in the very act of creation of these worlds, weaving their fabric with their words. So indeed: ‘Blessed are the legend-makers with their rhyme of things not found within recorded time’ (*TL, Mythopoeia*, p. 88) as they let us experience yet new wonders made by their artistry as did professor Tolkien himself.

Works Consulted

Kalevala – The Land of Heroes, trans. by William Forsell Kirby (London: The Athlone Press, 1985).

Translating The Lay of Aotrou and Itroun into French: across the Channel here and back again

Bertrand Bellet

The purpose of this article is to tell about my experience and present my considerations when translating in metrical form *The Lay of Aotrou et Itroun* by J. R. R. Tolkien into my native French.

I discovered the *Lay* in the early 2000s when a friend provided me with a digital copy. At the time, the poem was certainly known to exist (being mentioned in Humphrey Carpenter's biography) but could hardly be obtained in France; and I was thrilled to discover what was, to me, a hidden Tolkien treasure. I was then quite active on the French Tolkien website and community JRRVF – *J. R. R. en version française*[1] and especially involved in discussions about Tolkien's style and poetry. I was one among several people dissatisfied in the French version of *The Lord of the Rings* by the choice of the translator Francis Ledoux to paraphrase the poems line by line but into prose: in our opinion it did not work.[2] This led some of us to try our hands at something more to our tastes, and I

[1] URL: www.jrrvf.com.

[2] A second French translation was since published from 2014 to 2016. The translator Daniel Lauzon adressed this issue and translated the poems as poems – and fairly good ones in my opinion. He kindly credited those discussions of JRRVF and several of us by name for feeding his inspiration.

discovered in the process that I enjoyed the exercise very much and, more importantly, that my attempts were also sincerely enjoyed by others. This motivated me to endeavour something more ambitious, and an expected event then directed my attention towards a whole translation of *The Lay of Aotrou and Itroun*.

Tolkienmoots had just started being organized within the *JRRVF* community, and the next one was being planned in Paimpol, Northern Brittany, for May 2004. This was the perfect opportunity to present Tolkien's Breton lay to a French audience. I spent many leisure hours at it during the 2003-2004 winter and 2004 spring and was happy to achieve it on time. The attendants' feedback was very good, but this remained a private work for which I had no further immediate purpose, until I met Michaël Devaux, the editor of *La Feuille de la Compagnie*, a serial of Tolkien studies in French. He had heard about my translation, and, once he had read it, suggested to have it published in earnest. For various reasons, this is taking a much longer time that initially planned, yet I think this time has not been wasted. Throughout these years, my appreciation of Tolkien's works has matured, my knowledge of the *Lay*'s themes, context and mediæval models has increased; last but not least, Verlyn's Flieger edition of Tolkien's Breton poems in 2016 provided a wealth of welcome information on the poem's creation. This allowed me to reconsider more deeply my translational practice and principles (not all of them quite conscious at first) and to revise my translation accordingly with many small, and some more substantial corrections.

I will now first recapitulate the history of Breton lays, on the model of which *The Lay of Aotrou and Itroun* was composed. Then I will consider the formal characteristics of Tolkien's poem and how I found French equivalents for similar effect. Finally, I will discuss some translational questions related to Tolkien's poetic diction.

Lays in the Middle Ages

Lays are a rather loosely defined poetic form of the French and English Middle Ages. The word *lai* appeared in Old French in the second half of the 12th century. Its etymology is disputed: according to *Le Trésor de la langue française*[3], it is often considered, together with its Occitan equivalent *lais*, to be a word of Celtic origin, related to Old Irish *laid* "birdsong, song, piece of verse". A second explanation would make it a specialized use of the homonym Old French word *lai* meaning "secular, profane, civil, not clerical; common, ordinary" (from Latin *laicus*, itself from Greek λαϊκός "of the people, public"): lays would then have been characterized by their secular subjects in contrast with clerical poetry. A third option favoured by the *Oxford English Dictionary* would make it a word of Frankish origin related to other Germanic words used for various kinds of play: Gothic *laiks* "dance", Old Norse *leikr* "game, contest, sport", Old English *lác* "play, sport" and most to the point Old High German *leih* "song, melody, music", whose later Middle High German outcome *Leich* became applied to a poetic form very similar to French lays.[4]

The first lays, or *narrative lays*, are short stories in rhymed

[3] *Le Trésor de la langue française informatisé*, entry LAI². URL: http://www.cnrtl.fr/definition/lai.
[4] Alex Preminger, T. V. F. Brogan (editors). *The New Princeton Encyclopedia of Poetry and Poetics*. Princeton University Press, 1993. Entry LEICH pp. 686-687.

octosyllabic couplets that were sung to the sound of string instruments, and usually deal with thwarted love and wonder, often (but not always) in relation with the matter of Brittany. Narrative lays are characterized by a great simplicity of form, featuring a single, undivided story, and a noble tone, in clear contrast with the formally similar but comical and typically bawdy *fabliau*. Narrative lays are more like romances, although much shorter and less elaborated; indeed, they could quite pointedly be said to be to romances what novellas are to novels. Such lays appeared in the second half of the 12th century in the work of Marie de France, the first recorded female poet in the French language. Very little is known of her life, all of it inferred from what appears in her works: *Ysopet*, a collection of fables imitated from Æsopus; *L'Espurgatoire seint Patriz* or "The Purgatory of Saint Patrick"; and her twelve *Lays: Guigemar, Equitan, Fresne* ("The Ash Tree"), *Bisclavret* ("The Werewolf"), *Lanval, Deus Amanz* ("The Two Lovers"), *Yonec, Laüstic* ("The Nightingale"), *Milun, Chaitivel* ("The Unhappy"), *Chievrefoil* ("The Honeysuckle"), *Eliduc*. She wrote in the Anglo-Norman dialect and appears to have been associated with the Plantagenet court; she must have been born in France but likely spent much of her life in England.[5] Her lays were very popular and established the model for further compositions in this style, both in French and English.

The word *lay* was soon extended in France to different,

[5] This is inferred from a verse at the end of her *Ysopet*, from which also cames the name that we moderns gave her: *Marie ai num, si sui de France* "My name is Marie and I am from France". That it was distinctive enough to be remarked probably means that she had moved away from her native land. Her Anglo-Norman dialect and a few English words sprinkled in her poems are also indications.

more elaborated poems, with introduction of stanzas and more varied rhyme schemes. Themes shifted from storytelling to the expression of feeling in song, including religious feeling. Such lays are called *lyrical lays* and flourished in France from the 13th to the 15th century, with Guillaume de Machaut as the most famous master of the form. They were characteristically made of a variable number of stanzas, each with a different line count, meter and rhyme pattern, and each to be sung on a separate tune. With the introduction of refrains from the *rondeau*, lyrical lays would further evolve into the *virelai* of the French Late Middle Ages.[6]

In England however, the original narrative lays lasted longer as a form, as French lays were translated or imitated into Middle English in the 13th and 14th centuries. They are known as "Breton lays" in histories of English literature. Examples are *Lay le Freyne*, *Sir Orfeo*, *Sir Degaré*, *Sir Gowther*, *Sir Launfal*, *Landeval*, *Emaré*, *The Erl of Toulouse* or Chaucer's *Franklin's Tale* in *The Canterbury Tales*. Tolkien emulated this very tradition when he composed *The Lay of Aotrou and Itroun*.

I would now like to illustrate narrative lays by the two following brief extracts.

Marie de France, *Chievrefoil* (edition by Alexandre Micha[7], my translation):

Pur la joie qu'il ot eüe	For the joy he had felt
De s'amie qu'il ot veüe	that he had seen his beloved,
Et pur ceo k'il aveit escrit	and for remembering the words

[6] Michèle Aquien. *Dictionnaire de poétique*. Paris: Librairie générale française, 1993. (Le Livre de Poche.) Entry LAI pp. 166-167.

[7] *Lais de Marie de France*. Traduction et présentation par Alexandre Micha. Paris: Flammarion, 1994. (GF-Flammarion; 759).

Si cum la reïne l'ot dit,	that he had written
Pur les paroles remembrer,	just like the queen had said them,
Tristram, ki bien saveit harper,	Tristram, who played the harp well,
En aveit fet un nuvel lai;	had made a new lay of them;
Asez brefment le numerai:	I will name it quite in brief:
Gotelef l'apelent Engleis,	the English call it Gotelef ("Honeysuckle"[8]),
Chievrefoil le nument Franceis.	the French call it *Chievrefoil.*
Dit vus en ai la verité	I have told you the truth
Del lai que j'ai ici cunté.	of the lay I have recounted here.

Sir Orfeo (edition[9] and translation[10] by J. R. R. Tolkien)

Biforn þe king he sat adoune,	Before the king upon the ground
and tok his harpe miri of soune,	he sat, and touched his harp to sound;
and tempreþ it as he wel can,	his harp he tuned as well he could,
and blissfule notes he þer gan,	glad notes began and music good,
þat alle þat in þe palais were	and all who were in palace found
come to him for to here,	came unto him to hear the sound,
and liggeþ adoune to his fete,	and lay before his very feet,
hem þenkeþ his melodie so swete.	they thought his melody so sweet.
Þe king herkneþ and sitt ful stille,	He played, and silent sat the king
to here his gle he haþ god wille;	for great delight in listening;

[8] *Gotelef* is of course a Middle English form of "goat's leaf", a calque of Old French *chievrefoil* (modern *chèvrefeuille*) and its Latin origin *caprifolium.*

[9] *Sir Orfeo: A Middle English Version by J. R. R. Tolkien.* Edited, with introduction and notes by Carl F. Hostetter. In *Tolkien Studies: An Annual Scholarly Review* vol. 1, 2004. Morgantown (West Virginia): West Virginia University Press, 2004, pp. 85-123.

[10] *Sir Gawain and the Green Knight, Pearl and Sir Orfeo: translated by J. R. R. Tolkien.* Edited by Christopher Tolkien. London: HarperCollins, 2006.

god bourde he hadde of his gle,	great joy this minstrelsy he deemed,
þe riche quen also hadde he.	and joy to his noble queen it seemed.

Formal considerations

The Lay of Aotrou and Itroun faithfully takes over the two main formal characteristics of the narrative lay: the octosyllabic line (usually in the form of iambic tetrameters) and the rhymed couplets. But the poem includes several additional features that are not part of the tradition set by Marie de France. It is divided into sections of various length; they can hardly be defined as "stanzas" as they have no special characterization of their own (except typographically by a line break), and are rather logical divisions required by the progress of the story. This does not stray far from mediæval lays. However, Tolkien innovates as he regularly introduces interludes between narrative moments (which can include several sections) in the form of extra-narrative quatrains, which always remind the reader that the action is set in *Britain* or *Brittany* (treated as equivalent words), forebode the general tone of the coming sections, and often represent a break in the timeline. Although technically not refrains, as each of those quatrains is different, they use very similar wordings and clearly echo each other:

In Britain's land beyond the seas
the wind blows ever through the trees;
in Britain's land beyond the waves
are stony shores and stony caves.
(...)
In Britain's land beyond the waves

are stony hills and stony caves;
the wind blows ever over hills
and hollow caves with wailing fills.
(...)
In Britain ways are wild and long,
and woods are dark with danger strong;
and sound of seas is in the leaves,
and wonder walks the forest-eaves.
(...)
In Britain's land across the seas
the spring is merry in the trees;
the birds in Britain's woodlands pair
when leaves are long and flowers are fair.

Another addition is a highly frequent and sometimes even heavy use of alliteration:

*No **ch**ild he had his house to **ch**eer,*
*to fill his **c**ourts with laughter **c**lear;*
*though **w**ife he **w**ooed and **w**ed with ring,*
*who love to **b**oard and **b**ed did **b**ring (...)*

*In the **h**omeless **h**ills was her **h**ollow dale,*
***b**lack was its **b**owl, its **b**rink was pale;*
*there **s**ilent on a **s**eat of **s**tone*
before her cave she sat alone. (...)

*The **w**ay was long, the **w**oods were dark;*
*at **l**ast the **l**ord beheld the spark*
*of **l**iving **l**ight from window high,*
*and **kn**ew his halls and towers were **n**igh. (...)*

*The **w**andering **w**ay was long and **w**ild;*

*and **h**astening **h**ome to wife and child*
*at last the **h**unter **h**eard the knell*
at morning of the sacring-bell; (...)

However, alliteration is not systematic enough to be a structural element of the poem, unlike the many works that Tolkien put into of a modernized form of the Old English alliterative verse. Interestingly however, Verlyn Flieger's 2016 edition of Tolkien's Breton poems (*A&I*) revealed a "fragment" of 29 lines prefiguring the final *Lay* but using blank alliterative verse:

*Of **o**ld a lord in **a**rchéd halls,*	all. of initial vowels
*whose **st**anding **st**ones were **st**rong and grey,*	double all. with *st*
*whose **t**owers were **t**all o'er **t**rees upraised,*	double all. with *t*
*once **d**welt till **d**ark his **d**oom befell.*	double all. with *d*
*No **ch**ild he **h**ad to **ch**eer his **h**ouse,*	all. with ch crossed with *h*
*no **s**on nor heir to **s**word and land,*	all. with *s*
*though **w**ife he **w**ooed and **w**ed with ring,*	double all. with *w*
*and **l**ong his bed in **l**ove she shared. (...)*	all. with *l*

Therefore, it appears that J. R. R. first put this Breton-themed poem into a form derived from Old English poetry, not unlike the poet of *Sir Gawain and the Green Knight* who composed an Arthurian romance in the inherited alliterative verse (with some modifications). This may be regarded as a symbolic way for Tolkien to naturalize a foreign tale on English soil; more immediately, this is another testimony, after *The Children of Húrin*, *The Fall of Arthur*, *Sigurd and Gudrún*, *The Homecoming of Beorhtnoth Beorhthelm's son*, of his abiding love for the old meter of Anglo-Saxon England and his great effort to revive and adapt it to the modern idiom. Nevertheless, in the case of *The Lay of Aotrou and Itroun* he finally chose a form more in line with the French origins of the Breton lays, this time more like the poet of *Sir Orfeo*. He gave it a special cast nonetheless by using alliteration and echoing quatrains.

How now would I find or fashion a functionally equivalent form from the French poetic tradition? When I began my translation in 2003, some principles were already quite clear. First and foremost, it was to be a literary translation, made for the joy of reading, reciting and listening, therefore a thing of beauty before being a thing to study (this was before I discovered that the latter could also improve the appreciation of the former). It had to be a French poem "walking on its own legs", working as poetry without necessary reference to the original English. And to be a narrative lay, it had to respect the long-established form and use octosyllabic couplets.

Octosyllabic verse immediately revealed a major difficulty – space. Translators from English into French are well aware that their art empirically results in a longer text than the original. Poetry is even more challenging than prose in that respect, especially Tolkien's poetry, which may be quite terse and largely relies on monosyllabic words packed with sense and consonants, of which English has many, especially in its basic vocabulary. By contrast, French words tend to be less consonantal[11] but spread out on more syllables – even more so in poetry, where many words are phonetically longer than usual, because the traditional prosody of French verse requires to pronounce a lot of schwas that are normally omitted in the

[11] Especially in the inherited, basic vocabulary. Learned words of direct Greek and Latin origin are much more similar in the two languages but reflect the patterns of their sources rather than the native phonetic tendencies.

modern language (except in Southern France).[12]

I chose to solve this problem by expanding the number of lines by a quarter or so: the original version has 506 lines; my translation has 631. I have strictly kept the division into sections, which are the logical units of the story, but within sections I freely put the number of lines required by natural diction, and sometimes slightly reshuffled the contents for the sake of French syntax. Therefore, there is no regular correspondence between the original and translated lines. The quatrains however are an exception: I have kept them the quatrains much closer to the original form, because it allows them to still serve as echoes and reminders of the progress of the story. This came at a greater cost as far as accuracy is concerned, but I considered that their actual content of the quatrains, which is not directly relevant to the story but more of a counterpoint intended to set a specific mood, could sometimes be modified a bit without harm, as long as the mood was correct. Here are as an example the first quatrain and first narrative section, with boldface und underlining to pinpoint the correspondences.

In Britain's land beyond the seas
the wind blows ever through the trees;
in Britain's land beyond the waves
are stony shores and stony caves.

En Bretagne au-delà des vagues
Toujours il vente dans les arbres;
En Bretagne au-delà des mers
Sont côtes et grottes de pierre.

[12] Called for that reason "*e muet*", that is "silent *e*" or "*e caduc*", that is "lapsed e". In traditional verse prosody, a written *e muet* must be pronounced everywhere, except before or after a vowel, or before a pause (most importantly at the end of a line).

There stands a ruined toft now green
where lords and ladies once were seen,
where towers were piled above the trees
and watchmen scanned the sailing seas.
Of old a lord in arched hall
with standing stones yet grey and tall
there dwelt, till dark his doom befell,
as still the Briton harpers tell.

Il s'y dresse un manoir en ruine,
***Verdi maintenant**, où jadis*
L'on pouvait voir seigneurs et dames,
Où des tours dépassaient les arbres
Et des guetteurs scrutaient les mers.
Un seigneur** demeurait **naguère
En ces larges salles voûtées.
Où se dressaient grandes et grises
De massives pierres levées,
Jusqu'à sa noire perdition,
Ainsi que maintenant encore
Le content les harpeurs bretons.

Then came the question of rhyming. Rhyme is certainly more important in the French than the English poetic tradition. The first monuments of French poetry (notably the *chansons de geste*) did not exactly use it and relied on assonance instead (the repetition of the same vowel sound without consideration for the consonants), but rhyme later because nearly universal. Blank verse has been exceptional before the end of the 19th century. By contrast, rhyme was nearly foreign to Old English poetry, and blank verse has always remained important in English. The functional role of rhyme is also comparatively greater in French, which has less opportunity than English to play upon the contrast of stressed and unstressed syllables, with its light stress invariably falling of the last syllable of word groups. Instead, French poetry has long relied for structure upon a strict count of syllables and rhyme schemes, extensively exploring both their echo and variation effects. Traditional poetic lore (taught at school, for instance – as far as it is still done) has rather little to say about rhythm, but abounds in concepts for rhyme quality and schemes.

And yet I decided not to use rhyme, at least not regularly or traditionally so. Finding a rhyme every eighth syllable is very demanding, even if disregarding, like most modern poets do, several phonetically obsolete rules restricting acceptable rhymes in classical French poetry.[13] I soon found out that the rhyming couplets expected in a narrative lay were bound to turn into a Procrustean bed that would force me into unnatural syntax, contorted word choices or even pure padding just for the sake of the rhyme. Now while the *Lay* certainly uses a number of words and constructions that are no part of today's

---

[13] To be more specific, for readers with a knowledge of French: a big restriction is the *règle de la liaison supposée* (rule of assumed liaison), which requires that two words ending with mute consonants able to resurface in *liaison* only rhyme when the linking consonant would then be pronounced the same... except that it is normally NOT pronounced now at the end of a line because this means a pause. As a result, *premier* "first" and *dormiez* "[you (pl.)] were sleeping" are not allowed not rhyme even if both end in [mje] in most situations. Another rule prescribes to alternate feminine rhymes (ending in *e muet*) and masculine rhymes (others), even if e muet is not pronounced at the end of a line anyway; it also forbids a rhyme between "feminine" and "masculine" words that are now pronounced the same: for instance, *fils* "son" et *vice* "vice" both end in [is] but would not rhyme, neither would *vu* "seen (masculine)" and *vue* "seen (feminine) / sight" and hundreds of similar pairs fully identical in sound today. These rules are holdovers from previous times when there was an actual phonetic difference precluding a rhyme, but were artificially maintained by tradition well into the 19th century.

usual English, this not art for art's sake, but the way to set the stage in the remote "once upon a time" of fairy tales and Breton wonder, and serve what is primarily a moral tale. I was afraid that too much artificiality, especially in syntax, would harm the lay's narrative power, and, worse, sometimes produce comical effects completely out of place in so serious, indeed so tragic a poem than *The Lay of Aotrou and Itroun*.

This is not at all to say that I gave up on sound play. There remained many occasions where rhyme, internal rhyme or assonance came up without strain, and I used them liberally but not regularly so. Quite simply, instead of providing a structural element to the translated poem, they are mere embellishments, quite like Tolkien's alliterations in the final version of the *Lay*. I was thus able to evoke at least a phantom of rhyme without feeling restricted. I will use again the first quatrain and first narrative section to illustrate the point.

*En Bret**a**gne au-del**à** des v**a**gues*	
*Toujours il vente dans les **a**rbres;*	}[a] assonance
*En Bret**a**gne au-del**à** des mers*	
Sont côtes et grottes de pierre.	}[ɛʁ] end rhyme
Il s'y dresse un manoir en ruine,	–
*Ver**di** maintenant, où ja**dis***	[di] internal rhyme
*L'on pouvait voir seigneurs et d**a**mes,*	
*Où des tours dépassaient les **a**rbres*	}[a] assonance
*Et des guett**eurs** scrutaient les mers.*	}[ɛʁ] end rhyme + [œʁ] internal rhyme
*Un seign**eur** demeurait naguère*	
*En ces l**a**rges s**a**lles voûtées,*	[a] assonance + [e] crossed rhyme
*Où se dressaient grandes et gr**i**ses*	[gr] all. + [i] assonance
*De mass**i**ves pierres levées,*	[i] assonance + [e] crossed rhyme

*Jusqu'à sa noire perditi**on**,*	[ɔ̃] crossed rhyme and assonance
Ainsi que maintenant encore	–
*Le c**on**tent les harpeurs bret**ons**.*	[ɔ̃] crossed rhyme and assonance

As for alliteration itself, I used it of course when an opportunity was obviously at hand, but did not put much effort into it. It is far less used in French than in English, and probably less effective for lack of the latter's strong stress to emphasize the consonants. As commented by the French-American cultural historian Jacques Barzun: "French is a vowel language: that is the great principle to remember. (...) Whoever wants to learn to speak, or simply to read poems in French, must believe in the primacy of vowels and do something about it. In his famous *Elements of Rhetoric*, Bishop Whately approves the common English advice to speakers: 'Take care of the consonants and the vowels will take care of themselves.' In French, the exact opposite is true."

To sum up, I set up a minimal frame of octosyllabic verse and then used my ear and taste, rather than any pre-established pattern to be followed whatever the cost. This was enough in my opinion to produce a text that is immediately recognized as a poem, without imposing overwhelming constraints that would ultimately have led me not to translate, but to rewrite.

Poetic diction

I mentioned earlier that Tolkien's style in *The Lay of Aotrou and Itroun* used a number of words and constructions that are no longer found in today's English. A few of those features, notably excusrsions of the usual word order, are common instances of poetic license; but most are outright archaisms frequently used in Tolkien's poetry, as seen for instance in *The Lays of the Beleriand, The Fall of Arthur* or *Sigurd and Gudrún*. Although finding an exact translational equivalent for every archaism is of course impossible, French offers many similar possibilities.

The first means Tolkien used to create archaism are the very choice of words:

- long obsolete words like to *reeve* "to steal", *druery* "carnal love", *rede* "advise, counsel", that need to be interpreted in their context by readers who do not know them;
- old words that have now been replaced by morphologically more modern doublets, but are still close enough to be readily understood, like *frore* "frozen" and *agone* "ago";
- and a few specialty words of like sable as the heraldic name for "black", or the *churching*, a blessing and purifying ceremony for new mothers after giving birth.

All these categories can be reproduced in French, not seldom with cognate if not identical words; it helps much of course that the vocabulary of mediæval court life is largely common to the two languages, thanks to the heavy and long-lasting influence of French among the English nobility after the Norman conquest of England. It often proved possible to "revive" closely fitting Old French words, exactly like Tolkien used ancient English words anew; one has to make sure however that the context or the very form of the word allow the reader to infer its meaning. Examples:

- *Druery* is actually borrowed from Old French *druerie*, so I naturally revived the latter for the purpose. The word *dru* still exists in Modern French with the meaning "strong and tangled, of vigorous growth" but its mediæval figurative meaning of "lover, beloved" has been entirely lost. But the context of *druerie*, the "fee" that the witch demands from Aotrou, is clear enough to make its meaning an easy guess.
- I used *rober* to render *reeve*, both coming from a Germanic prototype **raubōną*. This is the Old French form of this verb (and of course the source of English *to rob*); it is not entirely foreign to Modern French, but the form in current use is the prefixed *dérober* – itself not that common a word, much less so than the usual *voler*.
- I translated *evil rede* by *mauconseil* which is no longer in use but still readily interpretable from *mau-*, an old variant of *mal* "bad, evil" used as a prefix and *conseil* "advice, counsel, council" which is thoroughly modern and frequent.[14]

Of course, not all of Tolkien's antiquities have an equally ancient-sounding French equivalent. *Frore* for instance is rendered as *glacé* which is just "icy, iced". Conversely, to set the tone I sometimes used archaisms in several instances where the original had a plain modern English word: so I used *rets* "snare" (more commonly *filet* nowadays), *breuil* "enclosed wood" (no longer used but still found in many place names

[14] Incidentally, a street in the 1st arrondissement of Paris is named rue Mauconseil. I think I got the word there; at least, I definitely had that name in mind when I put the word mauconseil into the translation (among other late corrections).

and in the common surname *Dubreuil*), *hanap* "a large goblet, especially in the Middle Ages", *ouïr* "to hear, to listen" (now *entendre* and *écouter*) or *oiselaison* "gamebird" (revived Old French *oiseloison* with a modernized suffix, making the derivation obvious enough). Most of those words have often been used and reused in translations of Old French literature and will be known or intuited by French readers.

Tolkien also made use of some archaic morphology, especially in dialogue. The old second person singular pronoun *thou*, *thee* regularly appears with its possessives *thy*, *thine* and the associated verbal forms in *-st*: e.g. *thou cravest*. The old third person singular in *-th* is also found: *my wife lieth in childbed, when it God doth please*. Long possessives in *-n* are used before a word beginning in a vowel: *mine own bed*. Negation may occur without auxiliary *do*: *I know thee not, Grieve not Itroun*. Reflexivity may be left implicit rather than unambiguously expressed by *-self* pronouns: *that lord in guise of joy him clad*. These features are likely to remind English readers of Shakespeare or the King James Bible, where they are commonly found. Here French offers less resources. The time equivalent would be to use the style of Renaissance authors, and this is the period where French begins to be readable directly by untrained modern readers; but the morphology of Renaissance French is already fairly modern, changes are more noticeable in syntax and vocabulary. Still I could use a dated possessive construction like *Itroun mienne* "Itroun mine" (today rather *mon Itroun*) and, most notably, historical variants of negative particles: whereas modern French uses *ne... pas* (with *ne* usually omitted in colloquial speech), I have preferred *ne... point* or just *ne*, which were once common and now survive as literary variants with an ancient flavour.

Another point to be mentioned is the use of a full panoply of tenses that are all but lost in contemporary spoken French: past historic (*il chanta*), past anterior (*il eut chanté*), subjunctive imperfect (*qu'il chantât*) and subjunctive pluperfect (*qu'il eût chanté*). However, using them (especially the first two) is still a normal, expected feature of written French, at least in the third person: eschewing them results in a distinctly contemporary style, but using them has no special effect. On the other hand, finding those tenses in dialogue (and therefore all their first and second person forms) is now very unusual, certainly because it is difficult today to imagine people actually speaking so. It sounds stilted and awkward, maybe donnish, and according to one's tastes either quaint or conceited. But most often it just marks the text or the setting as belonging to a former time.[15] I aimed at this effect and unashamedly used forms like *nous fûmes mariés* "we were wed" or *nous l'hébergeâmes* "we harboured him".

Variations away from usual syntax are as common in French as in English poetry. The two languages are typologically quite similar in this respect: both mostly followed a verb-second syntax at an earlier stage of their history (like Scandinavian languages still do, as well as German and Dutch in main clauses) but developed a stricter subject-verb-object word order in the modern period. There are nevertheless remnants of the former verb-second order in some set phrases or proverbs and in the possibility (or requirement) for certain inversions – typically with a literary flavour, because the literary language, influenced by the model set by past authors, naturally tends to

[15] Notably, those tenses were still in commonly use in dialogue in the classical theatre of the 17th century (with Corneille, Racine, Molière as chief exponents), which is still widely read and performed.

be more conservative than the spoken colloquial.

Tolkien was especially fond of fronting for emphasis, we even have an explicit comment of his about this construction in his n° 171 letter to Hugh Brogan, where he notes it as archaic but still defends it: *'Helms too they chose' is archaic. Some (wrongly) class it as an 'inversion', since normal order is 'They also chose helmets' or 'they chose helmets too'. (...) But this is not normal order, and if mod. E. has lost the trick of putting a word desired to emphasize (for pictorial, emotional or logical reasons) into prominent first place, without addition of a lot of little 'empty' words (as the Chinese say), so much the worse for it. And so much the better for it the sooner it learns the trick again. And some one must begin the teaching, by example.*

Accordingly, the *Lay* is full of lines like *though wife he wooed and wed with ring; thus counsel cold he took at last; his name she knew, his need, his thought; the thanks she took not, nor the fee; and rich reward then you shall pay; a feast he bade prepare him now; a merry feast that year they made; a cup of silver wrought he raised; glad was her lord, as grave he stood; a longing strong and sharp I knew; dim laughter in the woods he heard; no sight nor slot of doe he found*; and many more. This is a strikingly recurrent device of Tolkien's poetry.

Other syntactic variations are occasionally found. Tolkien used them more sparingly, possibly because they are clearer instances of real poetic licence, not "justified" by the fact that they once were a normal word order of English. It would seem that their purpose is often to have an appropriate rhyme.

- Verb put after its subject and object at the end of a clause: *yet if thy heart still longing hold; the lord his lance of ashwood caught; [they] to their lady no word spoke; why do they mourning make?*

- Adjectives put after their head noun, for instance in this passage: *as pale as water thin and grey / that spills from stony fountains frore /in hollow pools in caverns hoar*;
- Insertion of content between a modifier and its head noun (hyperbaton in its original meaning, though the term is often extended to all kinds of deviation from normal syntax): *though wife he wooed and wed with ring, who love to board and bed did bring; his darkened mind would visions make of lonely age and death*.

Finally, the *Lay* contains many strikingly formulaic lines:

- Parallelisms: *with other names and other shields; to snare the heart and wits to reave; the way was long, the woods were dark; her joy was come, her pain was passed; we do not know, we cannot say; her face so pale, her hair so bright; sad is the note and sad the lay.*
- Oppositions: *black was its bowl, its brink was pale; alone between the dark and light; the wine was red, the cup was grey.*

Translating formulas presented little difficulty other than becoming aware in the first place of their importance throughout the poem. Inversions are also found in French, especially in poetry. Swapping a noun and its complement was often natural enough to achieve, with lines like: *ténébreuse était son entrée* ("black was its door"), *bienheureux était son seigneur* ("glad was her lord"), *âpre et long sinuait le chemin* ("the wandering way was long and wild"). Sometimes I also omitted the copula altogether, producing hereby a desirable formulaic style: *long le chemin, sombres les bois* ("The way was long, the woods were dark"), *rouge le vin, grise la coupe* ("the wine was red, the cup was grey"), *triste le ton, triste le lai* ("sad is the note and sad the lay"). A few times I also used clefting, a common device in French, especially when spoken: *son nom, elle le connaissait* ("his name she knew"). Overall, however, I used inversions rather less often than Tolkien did in the original poem.

A provisional conclusion

My translation is to be published as *Le Lai d'Aotrou et Itroun* in the fourth issue of *La Feuille de la Compagnie*, together with a number of essays on the *Lay* – some original, some translated by Michaël Devaux and Aurélie Brémont and myself.

Works Consulted

Lais de Marie de France. Traduction et présentation par Alexandre Micha. (Paris: Flammarion, 1994)

Sir Gawain and the Green Knight, Pearl and Sir Orfeo: translated by J. R. R. Tolkien. Edited by Christopher Tolkien. (London: HarperCollins, 2006)

Sir Orfeo: A Middle English Version by J. R. R. Tolkien. Edited, with introduction and notes by Carl F. Hostetter. In *Tolkien Studies*: *An Annual Scholarly Review* vol. 1, 2004. (Morgantown (West Virginia): West Virginia University Press, 2004), pp. 85-123.

Aquien, Michèle, *Dictionnaire de poétique*. (Paris: Librairie générale française, 1993)

Preminger, Alex, T. V. F. Brogan (editors). *The New Princeton Encyclopedia of Poetry and Poetics*. (Princeton: Princeton University Press, 1993)

About the Contributors

Born and raised in Genoa, Italy, **Massimiliano Izzo** currently lives in Oxford, where he is employed as a Research Software Engineer in Tolkien's very same university. In his free time he enjoys playing air guitar, listening to old school hard'n'heavy music, and reading all things fantastic, mythological, and Tolkienesque. Member of the Tolkien Society since 2015, he acted as a speaker at the Tolkien Seminar 2016 with the contribution "Recurrent patterns of the Fall in Tolkien's legendarium."

Kristine Larsen is Professor of Astronomy at Central Connecticut State University. Her Tolkien-related scholarship focuses on scientific allusions in the legendarium and the evolution of the female Valar and Maiar over the course of his writing career. She is the author of *Stephen Hawking: A Biography*, *Cosmology 101*, and the forthcoming *The Women Who Popularized Geology in the Nineteenth Century*, as well as co-editor of *The Mythological Dimensions of Doctor Who* and *The Mythological Dimensions of Neil Gaiman*.

Szymon Pindur is a student at the University of Silesia, Poland where he studies English Philology translation studies with Chinese. He was born on 15th of February 1996 in Siemianowice Śląskie, Poland. His father chose to speak to him only in English ever since he was born. That has kindled his love for languages and literature, which later led to one of the greatest discoveries in his life, namely J.R.R. Tolkien. He fell in love with Professor Tolkien's works at a very young age, as he read *The Hobbit* and *The Lord of the Rings* at the beginning of his primary school. Throughout his school years he became gradually interested in all things related to Tolkien and his writing. The love of languages combined with the passion for Tolkien led him to choose to study English philology in which he hopes to pursue an academic career in the future.

Bertrand Bellet works as a medical and social information scientist in Paris. He discovered Tolkien's works in the late 1990s and has since been especially interested in their linguistic aspects: style, poetry, translational matters, and invented languages. He is to publish a French translation of *The Lay of Aotrou and Itroun* in the fourth issue of *La Feuille de la Compagnie*, a collection of Tolkien studies edited by Michaël Devaux. He has also translated Old and Middle English poems important to Tolkien such as *The Wanderer, The Seafarer* and *Sir Orfeo*. He has written some articles about invented languages for *Tengwestië* and *Arda Philology*. He and Benjamin Babut are the authors of *Glǽmscrafu*, a website that illustrates Tolkien's fictional and inspirational languages and scripts by sample texts with audio records, translations and transcriptions. He is a member of the French associations *Tolkiendil* and *Le Dragon de Brume*.

About The Tolkien Society

The Tolkien Society is a literary society and educational charity devoted to promoting the life and works of Professor J.R.R. Tolkien CBE. Founded in 1969 as a fan club in the United Kingdom, today The Tolkien Society has over a thousand members worldwide. We are friendly, fun and passionate in our mission to promote Tolkien to as wide an audience as possible while growing our fellowship of people who consider Middle-earth their home.

Membership includes a subscription to the Society's two regular publications. *Amon Hen* is our bi-monthly bulletin which includes news, book reviews, short articles, information about events and much more. *Mallorn* is the journal of The Tolkien Society, featuring scholarly articles and in-depth reviews from scholars supplemented by full-colour artwork from some of the best Tolkien artists. In addition to *Amon Hen* and *Mallorn*, we publish proceedings of papers delivered at our annual events as part of our 'Peter Roe' series.

As well as our wide range of publications, the Society hosts a series of events each year. On 3 January we celebrate the anniversary of Tolkien's birth in 1892 by encouraging fans all over the world to raise a toast to the Professor at 9pm their local time. 3 March is Tolkien Reading Day, marking the date on which the One Ring was destroyed in *The Lord of the Rings*. In the summer we hold our Seminar for serious Tolkien scholarship, usually in early July in Leeds. But the centrepiece of our calendar is Oxonmoot. Held in an Oxford college on a weekend close to Bilbo and Frodo's birthday on 22 September, we gather for a long weekend of talks, discussions, quizzes, food, partying, masquerading and great company. For any Tolkien fan, Oxonmoot is not to be missed.

To learn more and to become a member of the Tolkien Society visit our website at www.tolkiensociety.org.

Lightning Source UK Ltd.
Milton Keynes UK
UKHW02f1828080418
320686UK00005B/195/P